MW00721186

SAY IT
AGAIN IN A
NICE VOICE

Eveline Power
    PO Box 244 MERVILLE VOR 2MO

- can you forward to UK
when Canada clan have
finished with it
    - hope you enjoy

Lots of love

will.

SAY IT AGAIN IN A NICE VOICE

MEG MASON

HarperCollinsPublishers

HarperCollins*Publishers*
First published in Australia in 2012
by HarperCollins*Publishers* Australia Pty Limited
ABN 36 009 913 517
harpercollins.com.au

Copyright © Meg Mason 2012

The right of Meg Mason to be identified as the author of this work has been asserted by her under the *Copyright Amendment (Moral Rights) Act 2000*.

This work is copyright. Apart from any use as permitted under the *Copyright Act 1968*, no part may be reproduced, copied, scanned, stored in a retrieval system, recorded, or transmitted, in any form or by any means, without the prior written permission of the publisher.

HarperCollins*Publishers*
Level 13, 201 Elizabeth Street, Sydney NSW 2000, Australia
31 View Road, Glenfield, Auckland 0627, New Zealand
A 53, Sector 57, Noida, UP, India
77–85 Fulham Palace Road, London, W6 8JB, United Kingdom
2 Bloor Street East, 20th floor, Toronto, Ontario M4W 1A8, Canada
10 East 53rd Street, New York NY 10022, USA

National Library of Australia Cataloguing-in-Publication entry:

Mason, Meg.
  Say it again in a nice voice / Meg Mason.
  978 0 7322 9352 9 (pbk.)
  Mason, Meg.
  Mothers—biography.
  Motherhood.
306.8743

Cover design by Jane Waterhouse, HarperCollins Design Studio
Cover images: woman lying under open dishwasher by Alan Thornton/Getty Images; Pregnant woman in stripy dress by Justin Paget/Getty Images
Typeset in 11.5pt Bembo Std by Kirby Jones
Printed and bound in Australia by Griffin Press
The papers used by HarperCollins in the manufacture of this book are a natural, recyclable product made from wood grown in sustainable plantation forests. The fibre source and manufacturing processes meet recognised international environmental standards, and carry certification.

5 4 3 2 1   12 13 14 15

For the Magnets

CONTENTS

A NOTE ON NAMES AND DIALOGUE

The names in this book are occasionally real, but mostly they are real nicknames: Shab, Minky, Bitsy, Snooch and Nona. Conversations are reconstructed from memory, and the timing of some events has been compressed.

Joy is a job.

Lionel Shriver

1

BREAKDOWN BAY

THERE IS A SQUAT, GREY BOLLARD ON THE SIDE OF THE Cromwell Road in London, near where it turns into the Talgarth Road and starts to get properly horrible. It is one of a row, and I don't know why I picked that one for the worst moment of my life so far. I think, perhaps, it was the furthest I could get from our flat, eight months pregnant, on foot, at 5.30 a.m., before the elastic band of conscience snapped back and I crumpled onto the footpath. Conscience, and a mounting fear that running pregnant beside the A4 at dawn might draw the eye of passing motorists. I leaned against the cool metal and cried as hard as I ever had, not counting my last two years of high school, when hard-crying while listening to Tori Amos and looking in the mirror was my hobby.

It was August, high summer and just starting to get light. London was in the throes of a sickening heat wave, which turned bags of rubbish left on the footpath into soup, and Tube stations into giant toaster ovens. Our flat, part of a converted Georgian terrace, was on the ground floor of a treeless street in West Kensington. With neighbours above, below, on both sides and behind, it was like a pigeonhole for humans. Even with the windows closed, you could tell what kind of vegetables upstairs was chopping by the particular tenor of the knife on the chopping board, or whether next door would want a suppressant or expectorant for that variety of cough. In the airless heat of that summer, not the coughing, the chopping, the street fighting or indoor arguing, barking dogs or the threat of home invasion could induce an overheated gestator to sleep with the windows closed, which meant a 24-hour loop of noise.

I had been lying awake since midnight, when the man downstairs, an artist whose day job was filling canvas after canvas with *Lord of the Rings*-y style paintings of waterfalls and smoking so much weed, had come home with friends and started a party in the basement garden. Even the sound of slippers on grass out there would have bounced up what was essentially a brick lift shaft and straight in our bedroom window, so 20 stoners singing 'I get knocked down' was just a teensy bit not conducive to sleep. It was his eleventy millionth party since the summer began, and I lay in bed hating him, but not tossing and turning exactly, because I had grown so enormous from 1) bebe-making and 2) eight months of unrestricted baked-potato eating that I had to really psyche up for a roll over. Although the extreme fatness had made my eyes into little piggy slits, tears pooled on my pillow, turning the white pillowcase a silvery translucent. Four weeks out from giving birth, a person's tolerance for communal living, heat waves, bong smoke and 'Tubthumping' can really taper off.

'I hate it here. I hate it so much,' I whisper-yelled to my husband, Shab, who lay brooding but inert beside me. 'I can't believe we are having a baby here. We are already bad parents.'

He suggested hauling our mattress into the living room, but that put us nearer the communal hallway, where the partygoers kept punching in and out on munchie runs to Korma Sutra, the all-night Indian takeaway within staggering distance of our building. We lay still.

'Can't you please go and yell at them?' I pleaded.

'It won't help,' he said. 'They are so stoned, they don't get that they're being noisy.' Shab was trying to keep the situation dialled down and maintain peace with neighbours we would still live rammed up next to after this morning. I saw only inexcusable passivity and decided to fix this myself.

I have always been especially judgey of people who do private things in public, like kissing with tongue, arguing or opening their suitcase on the airport floor to redistribute its contents so that any passing person can see their hairdryer and shoes not in plastic bags. But something, natural restraint I suppose, ran out at that moment. The desperation, exhaustion and a diffused fear that had been building ever since I stopped work a few days earlier was about to turn me into a little bit of a public spectacle. Whether or not the conscious bit of my brain could articulate it, my body knew I was on the verge of something scary and important and I wasn't ready. Nobody was ready, nothing was right. I swung my legs over the side of the bed, pulled on Shab's T-shirt that lay on the floor beside the bed and wrenched open the sash window that looked down onto the West Kensington Festival of Weed.

'Shut up! Just shut up!' I screamed down to 20 suddenly upturned faces. 'It's five o'clock in the morning and people are pregnant up here.'

Had they switched from peaceful summer-anthem singing to throwing bottles at our window or screaming back, I could have got a proper thing going and made stabby-finger threats about calling the police. In fact, I'd already done that hours ago, but in our neighbourhood, noise pollution came quite a way down law enforcement's to-do list, after illegal pay-TV installations and knife crime. Instead of reacting in kind, the dopey throng fell silent for a moment, then burst out laughing. I stood in the window like a fat lunatic, with nothing else to say. Anger turned instantly to embarrassment, my blotchy face smouldering with deflated rage. And then one of the revellers, who hadn't smoked enough to dim his faculty for wordplay, thought of something clever.

'You got knocked up,' he started singing, 'but you got up again ...'

Did it catch on? Why, yes it did. His cleverly modified lyrics tore through the group like naked flame through a Rizla and I retreated from the window, attempting one last, lingering look of fury, which was undermined further by my getting tangled in the cords of the bedroom blind. Back inside, I burned with a kind of stifled loathing towards everything and everybody, which, because it had nowhere else to land, landed right on Shab.

'You are so — why are you just standing there? I can't stay here for one more minute,' I screamed, while pulling on a pair of leggings. Under or over the bump? It's so hard to know with leggings after 30 weeks.

'Calm down; I promise it's going to be OK,' Shab said.

'It is not. It's already not OK,' I shouted. 'It stopped being OK so long ago I can't even tell you. If you honestly think this is the perfect place to have a child, you are bonkers.'

Mmm, *he* was bonkers. I ran out of the bedroom, through the living room, into the communal hall and out the heavy blue front door, trying to slam it so hard it would split. I didn't have anywhere to go especially, so I just ran blindly towards the

Cromwell Road and a bollard that I'd never noticed before and would forever after turn my head away from whenever we drove past it. As soon as I had sat down on the kerb, Shab came around the corner looking for me. He could have ordered me to stand up and come home, or told me off for sitting so close to moving trucks while pregnant. Instead he sat down too and put his arm around me as I heaved and shuddered with hot, salty sobs.

'We will fix this,' he said. 'I don't know how, but we will fix this.'

'I can't go back there. I just can't have a baby in that house. I honestly can't. I AM NEVER GOING HOME.'

So that was us, sitting on the side of the A4 as the sun came up, raking patterns in the pools of gravel with our feet. Me refusing to go home. Him maybe wondering why my less-than-watertight mental health hadn't outed itself before he married me. Four years earlier: a warm, shiny day in Sydney, a chapel looking over the harbour. All our friends and family; me, 22, gorgeous, as thin as a drinking straw but with giant cans; him essentially indistinguishable from a young Matt Damon. If ever we look at one of our wedding pictures now, I will always point to him and say, 'And is that you or is that a young Matt Damon?' And he will always say, 'Well, those are my shoes, but looking at that strong jaw, I would say it's a young Matt Damon.' Long marriages are built on the repetition of that calibre of joke. They are also built on shared interests, and happily Shab and I share an interest in making life difficult for no reason. Or not difficult exactly, but righteously challenging — just hard enough to make us feel secretly a bit awesome all the time. Two weeks after the sparkly wedding, we packed up our presents and left for London, without jobs to go to, friends or any particular plan. Moving to London in your twenties is so much like having a baby later on. You're pretty sure you're the first person to ever think of it or experience all its glory and hardship. Others will follow you there, but you'll always retain a quiet belief that were it not for your pioneering venture they'd never have done it. My parents were living in London too at the time, in a flat opposite the side entrance to Selfridges. We set up base camp in their spare room, and, between sending out job applications, I tripped back and forth across Duke Street buying pie dishes and ironing boards and drying racks because I thought Selfridges was like London's Myer. I still have the £240 ironing board, though, so cost per shirt is nearly below a pound.

After maybe six weeks, one of my job applications led to a writing test, an interview, then a job at the *Financial Times*. I had no prior work experience except waitressing during university and a spell of telephone market research, where my job was to conduct surveys on behalf of a company that manufactured diarrhoea medication. It's hard to cold call somebody at dinner time and ask them for the particulars of their toileting, so I developed a non-direct opener: 'Hi, it's Meg from ___ ___ market research,' I would say. 'I'm conducting a medical survey and I'd like to know if you've suffered from any of the following in the last six to twelve months: headaches, dry skin, muscle pain or DIARRHOEA?' I'd hit that last word hard to really bed it down in their subconscious.

If the respondent was still with me after that — and they usually weren't by the time I'd used the word 'survey', let alone 'diarrhoea' — they'd answer something like this: 'Um, muscle pain, dry skin — oh, and headaches.'

'No DIARRHOEA?' I'd say. 'None at all?'

'No, none.'

'Not even *one* watery stool, just slightly looser than usual? The consistency of say —'

Dial tone.

I didn't put that job on my résumé, even though that flimsy little document needed as much padding as possible. The *Financial Times* was launching something called a 'website', which was going to have news on it. It was 2000, or 'the year 2000' as everybody called it then, and funding for anything internetty was everywhere. You could open any cupboard in any office in the city and pound notes would come gushing out. Remember when there were websites that would let you order a CD single or a small packet of staples, and a guy would drive to your house and deliver your purchase within the hour, with free truffles? That was the year 2000. There was money for everything, including 16 graduates who worked from nine in the morning until just after lunch summarising business stories from American newspapers and uploading them to the FT website, which to begin with needed the same amount of padding as my résumé. Eighteen months later the cupboard would be bare and we would all be made redundant — an event that I guess we should have seen coming since our job was to summarise business news. Looking back, we did see a lot of stories with the words 'tech' and 'bubble' in the headline, leading up to the day we arrived at work and found large white envelopes on our desks where computers had been. Until then we just kept typing, relying heavily on the AutoComplete function to insert the phrase 'which analysts believe is likely to burst' in every alternate paragraph.

My boss in the US Abstracts Department/FT.com was a gifted journalist from Manchester, who had some inexplicable gaps on his résumé, if you would call being sacked for on-the-job drunkenness inexplicable. He was serving time in online news jail until print would take him back, and he was the kind of pale, slabby Northerner who smoked so much that his skin was peeling off anywhere it joined to other skin — the crook of his thumb, where his ear became his face. He looked scruffier when he wore a suit than when he didn't, so his go-to work ensemble was suit pants and a fleece. When you said his first name, which ended with a hard K, and surname, Hunt, together really fast they merged to become the rudest swear word there is, but his father — also a pale, slabby Northerner — had called him that on purpose to make sure he ended up tough. Maybe that's why K'Hunt drank only beer and tea as thick and coppery brown as a lake in the Urals. I used to think, when I couldn't help it, that he must have urinated a kind of rusty jus.

I learned important things from K'Hunt. I learned that any time you're struggling to write a headline for a news story, use a variation of 'Huge Big Thing Goes All Funny, Shock' because that headline fits 90 per cent of stories. If it's a first-person follow-up piece the next day, you make it 'Huge Big Thing Goes All Funny, My Nightmare' and you're done. 'Huge Big Thing, My Shame' is only for when you're the one who made it go funny. He also invented, or at least popularised, the game Disco Biscuit, in which players take turns stacking biscuits on the turntable of a record player while it is going. Whoever adds the biscuit that causes the pile to fall over has to eat all the biscuits. Disarmingly simple — but imagine, seriously *imagine*, how fun that would be. All you need is a packet of Rich Tea biscuits and a record player in working condition.

K'Hunt's second-in-command was a giant lesbian with type 2 diabetes, who mainlined brownies from Pret a Manger, in flagrant disregard for what they did to her blood sugar, mood and subsequent ability to talk to us not like naughty infants. Her nickname, Type 2-I-C, really invented itself; and although I say lesbian like 'I'm so down with gayness and know all about lesbians,' I actually didn't know she was a you-know-what-bian until another colleague pointed out that her manner and appearance were, in fact, so lesbanese that she had become a parody of herself. She had tattoos on her thick, unshaven calves and a close-cropped haircut with a little tufty bit at the front; she wore army-surplus trousers to work; and nobody was allowed to say anything bad about Buffy. At my first work drinks, I asked her if she had a nice chap. To me, the only standout thing about her was that when, on my first day, she found me wandering the halls looking for the bathrooms, she said, 'Oh! I need to go too, I'll come with you,' so that I had to freestyle a side-by-side cubicle episode with my new line manager right out of the gate.

Apart from her unpredictable insulin surges and K'Hunt's preternatural gift for purposely falling down while making department-wide announcements, it was a low-intensity workplace that came with an excellent email address and zero stress. The salary wasn't anything, but it kept us in fleeces and tea biscuits, with enough change for the bus home. Our office was stuffed into a low-ceilinged, four-storey building near Old Street, the saddest, most depressing underground station I've ever been repeatedly lost in. The real *Financial Times*, the one printed on pink paper, is housed in the glittering glass carapace of One Southwark Bridge, right on the river. Because I was fast at my job and had found favour in K'Hunt's eyes by making him a series of to-scale masks of 'People in the News' by blowing up their etchings from the *Wall Street Journal* on the photocopier, he let me arrange an internship at Southwark Bridge.

I still didn't have many skills to offer the editors at OSB, since they didn't love to give their employees frights by jumping up from behind a carpeted desk partition wearing the heavily pixelated black-and-white face of Alan Greenspan like K'Hunt did, but I was 22 and fearless. Also, being blessed with a gen X vocational blueprint, I didn't consider myself entitled to do only interesting work for lots of cuddles and clapping, so I did anything and without complaining. I never actually filed or collected other people's dry-cleaning like in films, but I got a lot of yoghurt for one of the columnists and faxed stuff, which is really the same thing. I answered mail; I wrote the diary listings. I spent a whole day stacking heavy back issues of a supplement called *How To Spend It* on top of a six-foot filing cabinet. To reach, I had to stand on a swirly office chair in pencil-thin heels, so that I kept sinking into the padded seat like a drunk girl on a sodden racecourse. That I only fell off once is a point of pride. Eventually I started going out on interviews with proper journalists, and some of the kind veterans who could discern my air of longing gave me 'Additional reporting by' credits on their stories because I had sorted out their parking meter while they wrote or changed their printer cartridge. Later, when I still hadn't gone away, they shared by-lines with me so that I could pump up my résumé even more, which would become useful much sooner than I wanted it to. I was working for free at the paper, being paid by the webness, and doing five days' work at Old Street in three days so I had two days free for ambitious loitering at OSB. I was pretty sure that, being as openly desirous as I was, I would end up with a full-time job at the paper.

So, no. When I asked my boss at Southwark Bridge about a real job, he had me fill out proper application forms for the Graduate Recruitment Programme, and maybe because I wrote 'Selfridges' in the Interests section of those forms, or because somewhere in the building a consultant had just realised that paying people to rewrite news was an unbelievable waste of money, I was made redundant from both jobs in rapid succession, the paid one, then the free one. Being let go when your presence in the building isn't costing anybody anything is a special kind of hurt. Still, I had learned an important lesson there, which would stand me in excellent stead later. If you have nothing to offer except free time, aim to just not annoy anyone. Staying out of everyone's grill is a very acceptable KPI. I didn't have any work to do but I learned not to ask for any, especially more than once. A lot of interns wrongly believe that asking for jobs all the time will make them seem peppy and keen. But actually, most senior staff find having an unpaid workie standing sentry at their desk and emptying their bin into another bin every time they toss in a Post-It distracting. Better to suck it up, walk quickly everywhere and water the plastic plants until a salaried employee gets pregnant or dies and you can have their job.

After the *FT* made the strangely ill-judged decision to make me 'available to the industry', I think that's how they phrased it, I found another internship, this time at *Saturday*, a weekend magazine that came out with the *Daily Telegraph* and was printed on paper as thick and glossy as silk bed sheets. The British *Daily Telegraph* is not the same thing as the *Daily Telegraph* in Australia, which covermounts sun hats on Australia Day and tacks the words 'baby heartbreak' onto most of its headlines, whether or not there is a baby in the story. The British *Daily Telegraph* is properly smart, and for about five years in the middle of the 00s, upper crustlette Elizabeth Hurley appeared so frequently on its cover, stepping aside only for an HRH or particularly lovely hen, that journalists from other papers started calling it the Daily Hurleygraph.

Everybody who worked at *Saturday* was related to somebody who appeared regularly in the back pages of *Tatler*, if they didn't appear in *Tatler* themselves. The editor was the only foreigner, an East Coast American with arms as lean and sinewy as lamb back straps. She kept litre bottles of mineral water stacked in perfect half-dozens on her desk, and her heels were killer at a time when *Sex and the City* was still just two nouns. I don't remember her name; I just remember being terrified of her, the arms, the water, everything, in a way that made really watery saliva come into my mouth every time she walked past. The English girls I worked with on the research desk were intimidating in a whole other way. They knew how to pronounce the last names of the aristocratic families we wrote about, like the Cadogans and the Cholmondeleys (who knew it's pronounced 'Chumley' and not 'Chole-mon-dell-eeeee', as I sounded it out?). Whenever the magazine wanted to set up an interview with, say, Stephen Fry or Emilia Fox, one of the junior researchers I worked with would offer to call Mummy, who had done the casting on the *Vile Bodies* film and knew Stephen var-well. They didn't really need help from a 23-year-old antipodean who still pronounced Berkshire how it looks, so, again, I had nothing to do. Nothing. My computer wasn't even plugged into the internet, which meant there was no burning time on The Google, but I couldn't complain, since, as an intern, I was lucky to even *get* a computer. Most of the time, the first 30 minutes of an intern's already-awkward day will be spent working out how to sit nonchalantly on an upturned mail carton because there's not a chair for them.

Being at a loose end in an office full of busy people is like being at a nine-hour wedding reception where you don't know anybody, five days a week. You have to invent things to do, like becoming 'unofficial photographer' or walking purposefully through the crowd with a drink in each hand like you're looking for someone. At *Saturday*, my elected project was 'fake typing'. I did fake typing for six whole weeks, pounding away at the keys with a look of intense focus on my face. There's a chance, actually, that I self-sabotaged; that I looked so busy that nobody wanted to bother me with their research assignments. In fact, in a month and a half on the research desk, the only question I was asked by one of the journalists was an offhand: 'Does one have muscles in one's bosoms, do you think?' I took a break from the fake typing and swivelled on my mail carton, although I like to imagine that I held up my index finger for a second first, without looking away from the screen, to indicate that I just had to get this sentence down before I could attend to her inquiry. In real life, I probably started just a little because someone in the building had spoken directly to me. I put together a complete dossier on female chest anatomy, but without the aid of a modem cable, and by the time I had got my little manila folder all done, the journalist had moved on with her life and I was back to my mission-critical Word document. Side note, that same journalist once called in sick, citing as her reason a streaky fake tan, and nobody thought it was odd. But back to this story's obvious lesson: I wasn't annoying, and a few weeks later, my near invisibility earned me a job offer as features assistant, which presumably came with a salary and internet connection. Maybe with time, hard work and some tenacious social climbing, I could have become the head of the bosom-muscle research department at *Saturday*, but my patent dispensability there for all that time, coupled with the fact that the other girls on the research desk kept going out for lunch and pointedly not inviting me even though I sat in between them and had to lean forward in my chair so they could lean back and workshop a venue, had filled me with a kind of internalised misery familiar to high school fringe dwellers and people who one day bring a gun to work. Happily, before I had a chance to accept, word of my virtual nonexistence got around and I was offered a better job at *The Times*.

It was the real thing. With a desk all of my own, a photo ID pass in which I looked medium-hot and whole sections of a new weekly supplement to look after all by myself. It was a little bit exhilarating, walking through the newsroom every morning on the way to my desk with just one coffee instead of an intern's tell-tale tray of six, scooching past a reporter doing camera time for a news network in the corridor, and getting bitten by the paper mites who bred in piles of old newspaper stacked all over the office, so that I left every day looking like a real journalist, irritated and a little poxy.

My boss at *The Times* was one of the few female editors I've ever worked for who was not, as it's known in journalistic circles, 'a total bitch'. It helped that she was in her forties, a mother, and had already proven everything there is to prove in a media career. She was the news editor of a national newspaper by age 24, one of the youngest ever. She had her first baby at 27, her second at 29, and she took maybe 25 minutes of maternity leave each time. She told me horrifying stories about hand-expressing over the basin in the work bathrooms before interviewing important people, on three hours' sleep. She lasted like that until her children were toddlers, when suddenly, she needed to be home and stay there for the next decade. For ten years she produced special sections for the *FT* from her attic study so that she could, if not look after her two children, then at least be in close proximity while a kind immigrant looked after them for her. That we both came from the *FT* at around the same time, although not from the same salary bracket, was a happy talking point, and by the end of my first week, I had quite the girl crush on Spackers, as she was known by upper management.

In and out of work, Spackers had a knack for dropping pearls of wisdom into casual conversation, nuggets that all this time later still come back to mind as I move in and out of the life stages that she'd already completed. She once told me, 'You won't drink a beverage hot for the first six months of your child's life.' I didn't believe her — how could that honestly be possible? Just put the child down and drink your tea. A few years later, as I paced the living room trying to soothe my second baby and counted four untouched mugs of tea with cold slicks of milk congealing on the surface, I remembered what Spackers had said. 'Never try and walk fast with a child, because they need to pick up all the sticks,' she told me another time. I ignored that non sequitur at the time too, since I had never tried to walk anywhere with a toddler. The other day as I returned from a 45-minute trip to my own mailbox, holding a handful of twigs that had been passed up to me to look after, another Spackerism floated up from the depths of my memory.

She had so much knowledge to impart and she treated me like her protégée. Within a week of my starting, she moved me off all the snoozy administrative tasks that a junior gets lumped with, like answering reader mail and making up things for the interns to do, and let me write a feature. I had never written a proper story before and I took the same amount of time over those 1,000 words as George Eliot took on her first two goes at *Middlemarch*. When it was finished, I emailed it to Spackers and sat opposite her while she read it, my forehead prickling and a rivulet of perspiration trickling down my cleavage.

'Well,' she said as she looked up from her screen. 'It looks like I'll be working for you one day.'

It was the best compliment I have ever received, and I still keep it on a special velvet cushion in my brain, like a beloved pet, stroking it gently and feeding it treats when I have a spare minute. From then on, Spackers let me write all day — extended features, cover stories, news for the main paper, which everybody called the 'main book', so I did too — and suddenly, a goal I'd set for myself by the time I turned 30 was bumped up by six years. My only professional goal in life up until that time, actually, had been to get a by-line in a newspaper you had to pay for, nothing you could pick up for free at the station. Since I'd managed it by age 24 instead of 30, there was suddenly a wide open space in my diary.

Despite being treated like a delicate genius at the best newspaper in the world by a woman with so much more to teach me, I started to get, you know, a little bit bored. Instead of being grateful or shutting up, I let twitchy happen. I began to look around for something else to do. A trip, a chunky fringe maybe — to a normal person, those would be good circuit breakers. But I had a friend, Emily, who had got pregnant, and at six months, she looked smoking hot and was getting a bunch of attention. So, I know! Pregnancy! What a way to burn some free time. And I mean, a bump, how cute is that?

I don't remember a single conversation with Shab about whether getting pregnant at just-turned-25, when my career was only just establishing itself, was a clever thing to do. The upside of not overthinking the timing is that we were never a couple who squeezes each other's hands at a dinner party and says in a stage whisper, 'Shall we tell them? OK, guys … we're trying!!!' as though sexing each other on weeknights as well as Saturday is worthy of a real-life status update. Since there was no reason to think parenthood would knock me off my obviously upward trajectory, we just started to mess around. There was a holiday in Greece, I think, an accidental shortage of birth control and some hurried assurances that 'it will probably be fine. I'll be fine anyway if something happens.' Something happened. Right now I'm doing imaginary baby-rocking arms and making a wah-wah sound.

Here are some things I could have thought about before I got a bebe in me:

1. Where are you living?
2. What will you live on if your husband gets made redundant eight months after your baby is born?
3. Do you have any family and/or help in London now that your parents have moved to New Zealand, which is far away?
4. How old are you?

Instead of chewing over those nutty little subjects and giving the whole idea some time, six weeks later, I was doubled over outside the floor-to-ceiling glass windows of *The Times*'s main newsroom and, in the absence of a well-placed planter box, throwing up good and hard onto the cobblestones. You cannot imagine the splash back. Eight months after that, we were sitting beside the A4. Wah. Wah.

2

AN END, A BEGINNING

I DID GO HOME.

But not for two heavenly, air-conditioned days and nights, which we spent watching movies and eating peanut butter sandwiches at the Marriott in nice, not West, Kensington. We could still afford expensive fixes like that, and we needed 48 hours of muffled hotel-grade quiet to work out exactly how I was going to do the thing I couldn't now get out of, without ever getting back to where we just came from. It was Shab's idea to go home in baby steps. He waved down a taxi from the A4, told the driver where to go, checked me in and went home to get clothes, the peanut butter, toothbrushes and my book.

I was reading *Travels with Myself and Another,* by Martha Gellhorn, a journalist who was married to Ernest Hemingway for a while. I'm not saying you want to take life lessons from a woman who in her will stipulated that her adopted son could inherit her estate only if he'd reached a goal weight of her choosing before she died, as an incentive for him to shed that final five. But she said something in a diary entry written during a nightmare driving tour through Africa in the 1970s that, when I switched out 'Africa' and replaced it with 'having babies', caught and stopped me: 'The thing about Africa' slash having babies, she wrote, 'is that you cannot give up and take the easier way out because there is no easier or other way. It must be very good for building character. You have to go on, the alternative is suicide.'

As depressed as I undoubtedly was, as desperate and terrified as I still felt, there really wasn't anything for it except to go on. There was no easier or other way, and suicide, even I could see, would be overkill. After those two days and half a dozen back-to-back viewings of the Ashton Kutcher–Brittany Murphy classic *Just Married* on an in-house movie channel, we went home. Well, not quite. We did go to *a* home, just not ours. Shab put a call in to our friends Lizzie and Max. They were the most grown-up friends we had, only a few years older than us but so much more mature and stable that seeing them was a bit like socialising with our parents' friends. They had a two-year-old daughter already, another child in the making and a lovely terrace house in a leafy, villagey enclave ten minutes away from our little corner of urban decay. I was quite nervous of Lizzie; she seemed so much more together than me, but her togetherness made their home the perfect port in my storm. They said we were welcome to stay for as long as we wanted. I don't know what reason Shab gave for our needing to move out of our own house and two miles up the road into their converted loft, but since they are lovely and gracious and English, they didn't ask any questions.

I spent my days, although I didn't realise it at the time, work-shadowing Lizzie, a stay-at-home mother. Sometimes I snuck upstairs for a sleep or small panic attack, but most of the time I just watched as she went about her daily business, as confused and underfoot as a work experience girl. It was my first glimpse of a mother's life at home and I was intimidated by all the briskness and efficiency. She knew what she was doing and I did not. But instead of being clever and taking notes on how she filled her day, made friends, and took care of money, babies, herself and a husband, I pushed through intimidation into silent judgement. How very strange, I remember thinking, that Lizzie would make dinner at 9.30 a.m. How obsessed she seemed to be with getting a load of laundry done and hung out before she took her daughter to nursery school; what an unfeasible amount of time she spent chopping up fruit for people who didn't seem to want it.

Although Lizzie never sat down, she felt as though she did nothing, because she wasn't a lawyer any more. 'Nothing important anyway!' she said. 'I really ought to get back to work-work. I just haven't really … well, I just … the time hasn't …'

The conversation tapered off, or more likely flicked back to being wholly internal, Lizzie arguing with Lizzie in Lizzie's brain. I didn't understand why, if she wanted to go back to work, she didn't just *go* — and those housekeeping habits, they were just too odd. A year later I would notice, while making white sauce at 8.45 a.m., that I'd adopted every one of them, after trying and failing at all the alternatives.

Even if I had known to write down what I saw there, the fact is every woman has to discover how to be at home with children for herself. Whether she spends six weeks or the rest of her life as a stay-at-home mother, the early days are a solo voyage into the new world.

'I've found it!' she'll realise one day. 'The new world!' It is like spying land after so long at sea, only to find a million women already sitting on the beach. They could have given her directions but ultimately every mother must make her own way.

After a week at Lizzie and Max's, it was time to brace myself and go home. My due date was approaching and I needed to focus. I decided I would clean to forget. It wasn't nesting exactly, because nesting is an involuntary hormonal impulse that has you up a ladder wiping the greasy tops of your kitchen cupboards at

41 weeks. This was a more deliberate plan to keep moving and not think about things too much. I laundered and folded baby clothes. I made up the crib; I ate properly. I bought flowers; I went for walks around the Serpentine in Hyde Park and stocked up on organic sea sponges and baby bath wash from the health food shop. I tried to smile at the artist when I passed him in the street. And then one day, while I was painting the skirting boards and leaning down to reach an awkward corner, a torrent of liquid came pouring out of me. The following week, the same thing happened, and this time it was my waters breaking, not me wetting myself because I'd put a little too much load on my bladder while bent over, as a shift doctor regretfully explained the first time I'd turned up to hospital with my overnight bag.

In movies, labour turns really nice women into foul-mouthed weapons who hit their husbands and say 'You did this to me' and other uncharacteristically mean things. In real life, or my life at least, labour turned an often-mean person into the sweetest woman you'll ever meet. I was a doll; I was a *lamb*. For those 12 hours, nobody knows why, I've never shown more tender concern for Shab or spoken to him in more loving terms. Admittedly I was so wiped out on 50 different drugs that had a pre-rehab Lindsay Lohan been in that delivery suite with me, she would have been like 'Hey, *whoa* …' but honestly, the number of times I asked if his feet hurt from standing up for so long while my lady parts were literally rent asunder, I couldn't tell you.

Labour was kind to me, and I was kind to everybody in there with me — all three midwives who were brokering a shift swap while I was crowning, the gaggle of student doctors I had let in to observe my transition because by then, who cares if the door's even closed? I even delivered a druggy little thank-you speech to the doctor who had stood at the end of my bed supervising and eating a ham sandwich from a triangular packet while I bore down and delivered the most perfect human I'd yet seen.

She was the deepest pink, floury, wet headed. There is love, and then there is seeing your baby. Everything I had heard was true. I was sitting up when she was born, and she shot out and onto the bed without anyone holding on to her. What can I say? My pelvic muscles were only 25 years old. I was the first to pick her up, as though she was a dropped handbag on the King's Road. I looked around to see if anyone else in the room was going to claim her. But no, she was mine. She was so beautiful. I felt like I had seen her somewhere before. She cried a reedy, quavering cry, and I wiped her forehead and cheeks with my fingertips. For once, I didn't cry. There was nothing to cry about. She was perfect. It was perfect.

There was a reason, now, to do this well, not just because a photocopied handout from the prenatal clinic told me good mothers stay away from soft cheese and hot baths. I had to be good at this for the minky little child who didn't close her eyes for the first six hours of her life. Instead, she looked intently at

Shab and me and wondered, I imagine, how this was all going to play out. While we chose a name, we called her Minky because she looked, folded into the hospital blanket with two wide, dark eyes staring out, just exactly like a baby seal or a whale calf, something polar anyway.

Because it was a public hospital, we would have what the admittance material generously described as 'up to' 12 hours in the recovery ward before we were discharged. My mother threw good birthday parties for us when we were small, but the minute they were over and the last child was picked up, she would get a pair of scissors from the kitchen drawer and go around the house stabbing all the balloons. The final bang was your cue to stop feeling special. After half a day in recovery, the party would be over, and it would be time to go home. With my brand-new baby in her little fish-tank crib beside me, I felt like the centre of the turning universe, but the slap of the hospital's swing doors would transform me, instantly, into an ordinary woman with a lot of very ordinary days ahead. Nobody singing, clapping and taking photographs, just me trying to make life special now for somebody else.

I didn't mind the early departure, since the recovery room Minky and I were taken to had four other beds, four other mothers and three other babies. The fourth mother didn't have her baby yet because she wasn't in recovery so much as still giving birth. The hospital was overcrowded that day and there wasn't a spare delivery suite for this panting, sweating birther, who was forced instead to do stage-two labour in a room full of women trying to get some shuteye. I couldn't sleep but it didn't matter. I had Minky to look at. Shab had gone home, according to ward rules, so I sat up eating the white bread roll that had come on a tray with a saucer of sardines and a brochure about the importance of good nutrition for nursing mothers. It obviously wasn't referring to the five headless pilchards fanned out beneath cling wrap heavy with condensation — later, I guess it meant, and on my own dime, it would be good to eat right. Minky lay on my chest and some breadcrumbs fell onto her head like snowflakes. In the background, the labouring woman continued to emit a low bellow that spiked every three minutes with short, high screams. I had started with a birth plan too, all those hours ago, one that involved massage and no drugs and blah blah shut *up* already. A midwife quite soon suggested that since I was clearly not doing particularly well (the power-vomiting and blacking out gave me away), they would find a nice doctor who could spear my spinal cord with an instrument that looked just like a no. 5 knitting needle only sharper. Yes please! Where have you been all my contractions? So he did, and like I said, there was a lot of love in that room afterwards. The labouring woman in my recovery room, on the other hand, was pressing on with a birth plan that, instead of calling for delicious injections into her lower back, relied some would say too heavily on the analgesic powers of a mix tape and a candle from home. I think we all got a little post-traumatic stress disorder in that room.

Before Minky was a full day old, we were spat out of the sliding doors into a bright white early-morning haze. Had I known that whoever it was who brought me the sardines would be the last helpmate I would have besides my husband for months and years to come, I might have tried to stay longer. Somebody wise, maybe Oprah, maybe Gandhi says pain sits right in the gap between your expectations and what actually happens. Anne Lamott says an expectation is a disappointment under construction. I felt the cruel misalignment of should-be and actually-is for the first time when I opened my hospital bag after giving birth. Three months before, when I'd packed it, I had obviously thought I would be wearing home pre-pregnancy denim, when actually I would walk out in the same outsize Gap culottes I wore in. Also, in my heart or my head or somewhere, I decided that everything would be better once Minky came. It was, in one way. I had a perfect baby, and truly, that is the main thing. But just because of her, life and London weren't going to be cleaner and nicer to me than they were before.

Proof came in the hospital car park. Shab carried my bag; I carried Minky and walked to the car with the wide-legged gait of a recently dismounted cowboy. A strong wind had got up, and in the tightly packed parking lot, there was less than

31

a foot of space between our car and the next, a black Porsche, not brand-new or anything but still someone's Porsche. As Shab reached into the back seat to do something with the capsule straps and I waited on the verge with Minky, the wind caught our car door and threw it into the side of the Porsche, leaving a deep, silver gash along its flank.

Who cares, right? It's only a car and I just made a human! A beautiful, perfect girl human, and this was her first time ever outdoors! Just as Shab stepped out to appraise the damage, a woman with a spray of keys in her hand came running towards us shouting something that the wind carried away before we could quite hear it: '... what did you just ... happened ... more careful my car ... fuu ... !!!!' The plan I had already formulated, which involved driving away and never thinking about it again, was not going to work out. The woman was hysterical, gesticulating, confrontational. I clutched Minky and took a few steps back so Shab could insert himself between us and her.

'You think just because you've got a baby you can smash my car and not give a damn,' she screamed, jabbing at Shab with the fistful of keys.

'No, I really don't think that. I'm very sorry. It was an accident but I would like to sort this out later,' he said. 'My wife has just given birth.' I started to feel light with fear, almost liquid. Minky felt too soft in my arms, like she oughtn't be out yet. I wanted to stuff her back in. The woman kept up her tirade while the wind swirled newspaper around our ankles. When a gust picked up the edge of her jacket, I noticed that she was a few months pregnant. Why wasn't she being *nice* to me?

Shab insisted that we swap details and take care of things at a more convenient time, when Minky had say, notched up a full 24 hours of life. We needed to get the baby in the car and out of the wind, he explained, but as we moved towards our car, the woman got into hers, turned on the ignition and jumped it forward a few metres to block us. I started to cry. Minky let out a few sniffly yelps.

'Please, could you let us go? I would like to go home. I'm very tired,' I said with more even-handedness than I felt. As she redirected her stream of invective to me, I knew I didn't have it. I got into the car and she turned back towards Shab for another go. He shut the door on us, creating a windless, whisper-quiet bubble. I talked soothingly to Minky, while thinking new mothers ought to be allowed to kill people and get away with it at least until their milk comes in. Shab eventually talked her down and into swapping details, and we drove slowly, silently home. It was not how I imagined Coming Home from Hospital. In my mind it had involved more flowers, more friends, more *something*. I felt weak and low, like something had been taken from me. I have occasionally wondered whether a few months later, when that woman left hospital with her own child, her mind skittered guiltily back to the time she bawled out the mother of an hours-old baby for a stupid mistake. Whether or not she gave us a second thought, the incident had already demonstrated just how little special consideration adults give each other. Special Consideration, it turns out, begins and ends with girls who get glandular during the HSC. I would not be let off. In fact, life's ordinary horrors — a moment of car-park rage, gum on my shoe, a mean-looking mother smacking her toddler in WHSmith — would be more sharply felt exactly because I had a baby. I was never, keen-eyed readers will have noticed, anything close to thick-skinned, and if I let it, baby-having was going to take me through thin-skinned to somewhere like no-skinned. I already felt everything too much, and unless I changed something, unless I toughened up, the raw and shocking responsibility of being someone's protector, instead of another person's protectee, was going to kill me just right down dead.

There is a scene in the utterly depressment film *Mother and Child* that might have helped me, except that movie hadn't been made yet. In it, a new mother called Lucy is sobbing on the sofa while her newborn cries itself to sleep in another room. She is wearing a scrotty dressing gown; un-brushed hair is exploding out of her head. Lucy's mother, Ada, is folding washing, listening to her daughter heave and weep and complain about how much she doesn't love the baby, the baby's not grateful, she's too tired to live, there's no point feeding the baby because it will just get hungry again, yackety yack. Ada listens for a bit, then can't for one more minute: 'Oh, for God's sake, Lucy — you think you're the first woman to have a baby? Shit! What did you think this was going to be? Jesus! Stop whining and grow the fuck up. Get your act together and be the mother!' So simply put. Would that every new mother had a wise, older woman nearby to tell them to grow ... up. Since my mother was on the other side of the world, in New Zealand, Shab's mother in New York, and the rest of our family diaspora-ed in between, I would have to workshop my much-needed growing up alone. It was time to be the mother.

Mothers, though. Oh my. Those women with purses the size of meat trays that hold chequebooks and an entire deck of school photos; who make casserole without a recipe and get very businesslike around blood and vomit; who take the smallest, charred-est cutlet for themselves, and give you the heads-up when Dad needs to be left alone. Who wear Red Door, have wet hands more often than not and do not consider cooking *and* cleaning up afterwards the gravest injustice. Who read on holiday and sleep on Saturdays, shout 'Mind my tea' with Tourette's-like frequency, make the tightest bed you'll ever sleep in and only swear under extreme duress, and even then it's more likely to be 'bloody hell's bells' than 'fuck'. Who drive hatchbacks, hand out worming tablets and disappear for six hours between nine and three, nobody knows where, but she sure sounds busy. How, *how*, would I go from me to that?

I would begin with a small dose of indispensable and go from there. Minky needed me, right then in the car park, and I had to believe that the permission slips, meatloaf and the tissue tucked inside the sleeve of my cardigan would follow. I would keep it together, all for her.

There is an upside to that car story, and it is this: the other car, the one we drove home in. We didn't own it, and since somewhere in the back of our minds we were planning to leave London soon, it didn't make sense to buy one before Minky was born. Oh, but imagine, a baby, a packed bus and a stroller that I didn't know how to work. A baby on the Tube; I had once, on the way to work, sat beside a mother and her baby, who was strapped into a buggy. While his mother reached into her bag for a minute, the baby leaned out of the stroller and gave the handrail a nice, long, lingering lick. Then he clamped his mouth around it sideways and ran his lips up and down, like it was a buttery cob of corn. I looked on in horror. No baby of mine was going to suck the pole between Cannon Street and Blackfriars. The very thought of it would make me burst my stitches. I'd been angsting about our carlessness to my petite circle of chums ever since a homeless person spat on my ankle while I rode the 28 to a prenatal appointment. Word that we needed a *voiture* for a little while got around, and one day, just a few weeks before Minky came, a friend offered to lend us his little perfect Peugeot matchbox. He was a jobbing West End actor who lived mostly off residual cheques from the *Mamma Mia!* soundtrack while he auditioned for parts. He was 'between money' at the time, he said, so if we made the repayments on it for him, we could have it for as long as we wanted. More than anything in the weeks that followed Minky's birth, that little sky-blue hatch would become my lifeline. My intravenous hope, my everything's-going-to-be-OK. No matter how tired I was, how much bong smoke had wafted up through the floorboards that day and formed a misty cloud over Minky sleeping in her crib, I could always get into that car, with a baby, a thermos and a book, and drive.

3

ALL MY SINGLE LADIES

I COULD HAVE *SWORN* I HAD FRIENDS BEFORE I HAD BABIES. I would have staked my borrowed Peugeot on it. Afterwards I felt like Robinson Crusoe right after man Friday blocked him on Facebook. It seems obvious now that if you have a baby at 25, in an even-slightly First-World bit of the First World, you will be something of a pioneer in your peer group. Friends my age were nowhere near procreation, mostly still single, working fun jobs for impossibly low salaries, travelling around Europe on credit, 100 per cent convinced that turning 30 would never happen to them. Apart from Emily, all the women I knew with children — workmates who had fallen pregnant and disappeared from the office or women I met in passing at Lizzie's — were already in their mid-thirties. But like the questions of accommodation, funding and emotional preparedness, I just skipped over that factoid and set about creating a new world for myself in which I'd have nothing in common with anybody. Too young for the mothers, too mumsy for my child-free friends.

Even for Snooch, my best pre-bebe-single-lady friend. We met in our first term of university and became inseparable. Soon after Shab and I moved to London, she followed, although she would never have thought to if we hadn't invented it. She is everything you want in a semi-grown-up BFF — funny, kind, an unflinching optimist who is sloppily generous with her money. She came to London to intern at the *Evening Standard*, a job she got, I still believe, because when the editor asked her why she'd make a good intern, she couldn't think of a proper reason, so smiled with bright, wide eyes and said, 'Because I love life!' How could you not hire somebody who loves life?

We saw each other nearly every day in our first years in London and each made important decisions — when to eat, what to wear — based on the other. We went to galleries together and spent eight minutes looking at art and two hours in the gift shop. We took day trips out of London and got bored looking at stately houses at the exact same second. We took the train to Paris together for weekends, where I would buy books from Shakespeare & Company and she would buy wheels of cheese so pungent we had tight conversations over whether or not it was OK to carry them around all weekend and then home on the Eurostar, so that whenever she unzipped her luggage, passengers nearby looked under their seats for things decomposing. I say, not OK. We visited Stonehenge once too, for a reason neither of us can recall since there is no gift shop there, only stacked-up rocks. We stood looking at them behind two American girls the same age as us.

'Wow,' said the first one, who was happy to be impressed.

'I know,' said her friend, who wasn't. She wanted to be an authority, even if it was her first time in England too. 'And Europe is just like this. Only … more so.' It was months before Snooch and I stopped adding 'only more so' to everything we said.

It was the perfect friendship, only more so, until I had a baby. Our relationship shuddered, then screeched to a halt like the train pulling into Waterloo. Snooch became, as single friends do to new mothers, the final word in mixed blessings. In one way, she was my fastest route back to the outside world. I could arrange to meet her after Shab got home, and see a movie or drink champagne in a tiny bar, confident that the chance of her wanting to talk about mastitis would be almost zero. I could take a deep draught of adult conversation before sinking back down to the sea floor of baby-having. Just as often, I would leave feeling stunned, *stunned*, at the unbelievable depths of selfishness and egotism she had started to display with no apparent compunction. She would be late. She would cancel at the last minute, bring a boy along or try and look at the time on her phone as I rounded out my second hour of uninterrupted mastitis talk. Three months earlier, I wouldn't have minded any of it, but now it was different. Her lateness meant a delayed feed and 20-minute crying jag for mother and daughter. A last-minute cancellation meant my torturous pre-date date with a dishwasher-hot breast pump had been in vain, and for the 33 seconds it took to empty a bottle of hard-won milk down the kitchen sink, I would silently rage against her.

After a handful of failed evening ventures, I decided we would meet only during the day and I would bring Minky, so the lateness would matter less. Even then, I couldn't make the investment pay. A few weeks out of hospital, I agreed to an overambitious trip to Selfridges. Snooch would pop out during her lunch hour and I would stow a still-floppy-necked Minky in the BabyBjörn while we browsed. She was 15 minutes late, which is nothing really, unless your entire day is carved up into 90-minute windows between feeds, in which case 15 minutes is desperately significant. I made laps of the Clinique counter while I waited for her. Minky began to stir in a threatening sort of way, like she may erupt at any minute, and I started to wonder if we'd made a bad call in coming. I walked faster. I bounced. I tried rolling back and forth on the balls of my feet. I tried swaying from side to side, making soothing noises. I tried a full set of lunges to keep the crying at bay. I was tired, of course, and a bit low on blood sugar, and by the time Snooch arrived, I needed a bathroom. I said a pinched sort of hello and while she went off to try eyeliners, I went to find the ladies room.

In the queue, I realised I didn't know how to use the bathroom while wearing a BabyBjörn. I had never tried it before. Did I take Minky out and lay her on a nest of paper towels I made on the floor? Did I try it with her still attached, holding her legs out of the way? Did I ask one of the women behind me to hold her for a minute, knowing with 100 per cent certainty that the woman would abduct her? Or did I (yes, I *did*) exit Selfridges immediately, bladder pounding, baby now crying, and text Snooch from Oxford Street to say, 'have left. speak later. so sorry.' I felt flat and guilty all the way home, like I'd done something terrible. At the same time, I was incensed that my closest friend thought I could manage an outing equivalent in logistical terms to a lunar expedition. It is not impossible that Snooch and I texted the same message to a third party on our separate trips home: 'ugh, she has *no* idea.'

A year before Minky was born, the author Rachel Cusk published a book called *A Life's Work*. The press eviscerated her for what really boiled down to a bit of honesty about how hard and lonely all this baby-having can be. Shab gets anxious when I read very dark books about the female experience, because I do tend to take it out on him afterwards, as though he is the patriarchal everyman responsible for whatever miseries took place inside.

'Locked in a loveless marriage and forced to give up her only child,' he'll read out loud from the back cover. 'Man, I'm going to pay for this later.'

And there was Cusk on an early attempt to take her newborn out for a walk through the park with one of her single friends. The outing goes extremely well to begin with until, probably high from the chat and impressed with her own managey-ness, Cusk overplays her hand. She suggests coffee at the park café, and suddenly ordering, chairs and baby-carrier straps enter the equation. As rain clouds start to form above their outdoor table, the baby starts to cry and Cusk knocks over her coffee while trying to ram the baby back into the pouch and, it's safe to assume, keep up an unbroken stream of chitchat with her embarassed friend. A few pages later Cusk is running through the park to a taxi with the baby in her arms and the pouch hanging open like the bib of some overalls undone.

In the normal old world, a walk in the park is a *walk in the park*, but in the new world I'd just discovered, where Cusk lived already, small outings and formerly straightforward friendships are impossibly complicated. With a baby now, your time and attention are so utterly required by one person, they become costly things that you cannot give away. As Cusk sped away in the cab, her friend waving bewildered from the kerb, she felt as though she had acquired her own sort of maternal taxi meter. Her friends might want to see her, but every minute would cost somebody dearly.

Snooch could not afford me and I couldn't afford her either. Having a baby had made me a Highly Sought After Person. Everybody wanted a piece of me, or at least one baby wanted all the pieces, so any piece Snooch took was snatched right out of the tiny fist of another. I decided to bench my best friend. It wasn't worth feeling bad all the time, the apologies, resentments and misunderstandings. Had I followed through, it would have been a merciless decision that only somebody addled by hormones could have felt justified in making after so many years of friendship. As I sat on my sofa feeding Minky and intentionally not calling, I thought about the flip side of cost: value. I loved our chats. I loved when she came over and cooked in my kitchen. I loved watching her talk to Minky in funny voices and eliciting early, precious smiles. I loved it when she held up one of Minky's hand-sized singlets while I sat folding laundry, and said, 'Imagine, no *imagine*, this was your singlet,' drawing my attention back to the overarching wonder of the whole business.

Snooch was also a bit magnificent at larger-scale interventions. When I found out I was pregnant, I made a firm and entirely unnecessary decision to make do without any proper maternity clothes. It wasn't to be frugal; it was to dazzle others with my ability to sidestep Tencel maternity jeans and continue dressing as though nothing out of the ordinary was happening girth wise. Quite often, I set goals for myself as though there is some sort of prize and recognition of awesomeness at the end, when in fact there is not. Nobody would even notice, or at least not in the way I wanted them to. Instead of hooraying me for clever sartorial choices, they would more likely look at the fly of my jeans, held together with a hair elastic and cleaving unattractively across a pregnant stomach, and wonder why I didn't just go and get some of those proper trousers with the stretchy welt. At around 30 weeks, Snooch suggested we draw a line under the misguided denim experiment and go to the Gap. She stationed me in the changing room and ran in and out with size after size, a hundred different styles and combinations. When we settled on a few options, she made me keep them on, tore the tags off, and went and paid. She stuffed the outfit I'd been wearing into the rubbish bin under the counter, and I left feeling like a hundred dollars. No-one but a proper, committed bester could stage a rescue like that. I finished Minky's feed, kissed her on the head.

'Shall we keep her, Minky?' She looked at me and the corner of her mouth drew up in a tiny, windy smile.

'Well, that's that then, I suppose,' I said. 'But no more Selfridges.'

All these years later Snooch is still at it, the rescuing. I am so glad about that right now as I sit typing with my nine usable fingers. A month ago I was standing at the kitchen counter bamixing crumble mixture to which I'd added too much butter. It was 5 p.m., children's dinner hour. In houses all over the country, women just like me were frying chipolatas in hot skillets while holding toddlers on their hips, flicking on food processors with wet hands or draining saucepans full of steaming pasta shapes while standing up breast-feeding. If I ever become an occupational health and safety warden, children's teatime is when I shall conduct all of my raids.

Crumble topping had got gummed up behind the blades, and without stopping to unplug the handheld blender or even really turning it off, I thrust my finger into its inner workings to dislodge the clump. I heard a thwack. The blade came to a graunching halt. Like a car trapped in mud, it whirred and strained against a fleshy impediment, 240 watts of mechanical fury vs my index finger. I pulled my hand away. The bamix fell to the floor, bucking and rearing like an injured snake. I wrapped my hand in a tea towel, and pressed my eyes shut.

I am, it should be noted, amazingly OK by now with every kind of liquid a human body can manufacture, except blood. Literally any other fluid I can face down and clean up without flinching, just not blood. My finger began to pound. I opened one eye to take a tentative look at it, but as soon as I saw the bench top, I clenched it back shut. It looked like there had been a tiny murder. I let myself slide down the front of the cupboard and onto the floor, squeezing my finger in the tea towel, through which a large crimson patch was starting to emerge. 'Ahhhhhh. Ahhhhahhh. Ahhhhha,' I sobbed into my sleeve, now unable to look even in the direction of my hand, although I felt desperate to know if I would ever be able to point or text or achieve a really smoky eye again. I imagined the tip of my finger hanging off backwards like the lid of a Zippo lighter.

I took some shallow breaths and called Shab. Voice mail. Minky wandered into the kitchen. Her eyes fell on the bamix now hanging limply from the socket. She saw the blood spattered up the walls and over the counter, saw her mother balled up on the kitchen floor with a blood-stained rag around her hand, moaning and trying to dial a BlackBerry with her foot. Her eyes widened, then narrowed.

'Can I have something to eat?' she asked.

I scrolled down to the Snooch's number and pressed the call button with my toe, wondering whether I would need to learn to paint this way. There could be calendars and greeting cards if I got very good. I would sell them and use the money to buy prosthetics.

'Snooch,' I sobbed as soon as she answered. 'I am OK, I just need to talk to you for a minute. I've had a bit of an accident and I feel a bit funny.'

I explained what had happened and she said it was probably totally fine. Always less blood than you think there is, she said.

She prescribed frozen peas and a lie-down. Keep it above your head, she said, keep the pressure on it.

'OK, OK. I will,' I sniffed, knowing that although these were excellent instructions, somebody still needed to sort dinner, bath time and bed. With Shab off-air, that somebody would be my micro-surgery-requiring self. I hung up and tried to wipe down the counter top with the elbow of what I had already begun to think of as my 'good arm'.

Twenty minutes later, on to my second tea towel and wondering whether you can put a blood transfusion on a credit card, somebody knocked on the front door. I limped unsteadily down the hallway, even though, strictly speaking, a messed-up finger doesn't cause limping. It was Snooch. With $75 worth of gauze, Betadine, sterile swabs, tubey bandages and painkillers in one bag, and a cooked chicken in another. She steered me towards my bed, set Minky up with both drumsticks and her iPhone, and came back to administer nurse-ly care, even though a) Snooch is not that into blood herself and b) the screen of her phone would ever after bear the faint track marks of Minky's chickeny fingers.

'Yep, it's not great,' she said, having prised the tea towel off me. 'I'll stay until Shab can take you to the hospital.' She sat chatting about intentionally distracting things and stroked my hair while I inched further and further across the bed, trying to get away from my own bloody extremity.

Every time I catch sight of the fiery-red scar yet to fade, I remember the learning: don't ditch your best friend, ever. Even if she is in a completely different life stage; even if she has better clothes, a flatter stomach or is late sometimes. One day she'll turn up early, uninvited, and just when you need her. Three months after Minky was born, a better job and a nice boy took Snooch away from London and back to Sydney. For somebody who had once been near to calling time on our friendship, I was crestfallen. I drove her to the Heathrow Express and made a moist, choky speech about how much I loved her and would miss her and was so sorry for being so boring and preoccupied and …

'Don't worry, you'll be home soon too. I'll get Sydney all ready for you,' she said. 'It will be beautiful.'

'Only more so,' we both said at once.

We hugged goodbye on the footpath while Minky slept in her car seat. I drove home not knowing when I would see Snooch next, and worse, whom I would see instead. The flat, when Minky and I returned to it, felt emptier than ever. A pile of laundry waited to be folded. I set Minky down on my bed and pulled a tiny vest off the top of the pile. 'Imagine, Minky,' I said, 'imagine if this was your singlet.'

4

THE PERCH

THE TITLE 'STAY-AT-HOME' MOTHER IS FOR ME, ANYWAY, A cruel misnomer. In two out of three ways, it's inaccurate, and I'm only allowing the 'at' because I'm too tired to argue with a preposition. In the first instance, 'stay' has no place in my job title. I've never been a percher, whose best topic is staying at home all day doing bits of nothing and eating half a banana. I've never woken up and thought, 'I might tackle the hall cupboard today,' and stayed in doing just that. Since having a baby, my special brand of outdoorsy-ness has only got worse, so that in seven years, I've never stayed home for longer than a single day-sleep. One or two hours is the longest I last inside with a child, unless one or both of us is asleep. So desperate did motherhood make me for adult communion and a little sun on my face that poor Minky spent most of her early life strapped into a capsule on her way to or from Kensington Gardens. We drove; we walked around the gardens; I read the paper in the car while she slept. I fed her in the front seat. Anything to avoid long, blinds-drawn hours at home, because crueller than the 'stay' for me was the 'home'.

That West Kensington flat was not the kind of home befitting an actual, occupational Homemaker. Describing myself as a stay-at-shitty-flat mother would have been more accurate, but possibly too confronting a way to introduce myself at parties. The kind of home I'd always imagined myself mothering in was all polished wooden floors, jars of full-blown roses and an expensive sofa I could afford to be nonchalant about. I'd have a dog. And I'd let the dog sit on the sofa so that when friends popped in, I'd have to clap my hands and say 'Scoot!' in a faux-exasperated tone that said 'Can you believe this guy?' as he padded off to lie in a patch of sun in the kitchen. Circa 2003, the only dogs in my life belonged to the neighbour on our right, who bred non-pedigree dachshunds in his first-floor bedsit and every morning let a fluctuating number of sausage dogs outside onto the footpath to produce small brown replicas of themselves on my front steps.

One day, our actor friend had borrowed his car back to get to a *Starlight Express* audition, so Minky and I had to take the Tube. As we sat waiting to pull out of West Kensington station,

I listened to a well-dressed American couple, tourists I suppose, chatting quietly to each other in the seats opposite. They were looking out the train windows at the long rows of terrace houses, which backed onto the tracks — houses just like ours. The wife squeezed her husband's hand and said: 'We are *so* lucky.'

'I know,' the husband said. 'We really are.'

My friend Allie I envy for two reasons. One: she invented a show-stopping recipe for taco soup, which is made entirely out of canned goods. Two: her surroundings don't affect her mood. I know! She can wake up anywhere, place her bare feet directly onto lino tiles or nylon carpet, and set about having a nice day. I only need to glance at a pile of smudgy DVDs sitting on top of their dusty cases and I want to fill my pockets with stones and wade into the Ouse. The flat's ability to bring me down has already been demonstrated via the A4-sitting incident, but let's put some meat on that bone. Let's lay out the precise chain of bad decisions that led me to purchasing the worst house in a worse street in the first place, and then I'll paint you a little word picture of the four walls I spent the first year of Minky's life plotting our escape from.

We'd only lived in London a few weeks when my brother, who had moved there two years earlier and falsely believed we had 'followed' him there, offered to lend us the deposit for a flat. My brother is a person so intelligent, so self-reliant and so adept at making prudent life choices that our parents openly call him Golden Boy. I think let's just be out with it and call him The Smart One. When we arrived in London, he was about to start a PhD in economics at Oxford, although his having a spare £20,000 in his bank account at age 24 makes me think there wasn't much more he had to learn, economics-ly speaking.

I always wondered why, since we shared a gene pool, Golden Boy managed to bags a much larger share of the available intellect, all the book smarts, the street smarts, the fiscal know-how, the lateral thinking and foresight, leaving me with 'quite good at drawing'. Then, one weekend on the phone to my mother, I described how I'd seen a woman at the doctors' fish a set of flash cards out of her purse for the twin babies beside her in their stroller and use the 20 minutes of waiting time to run through some basic addition and subtraction.

'So ridiculous,' I said. 'Can you imagine, trying to hothouse babies like that? As if it makes any difference anyway!'

'Mmm,' my mother murmured, agreeing but not quite. 'I did flash cards with your brother. But when I had you, I couldn't really face it so I just left you to it. You seemed very happy drawing.'

Since I can't make my brain work like his, I've thought about starting a blog instead, called Smart Things My Brother Says That I Would Never Think Of dot blogspot dot WordPress dot TypePad. The first post would tap this piece of Golden Boy's golden wisdom: if you find yourself having the same conversation with different people more than once a week, alter the circumstances that precipitate it. For example, if your name is Bridget but your parents were fruity and spelled it Brïddjitte, so that every few days you have to spell it out over the phone or explain your parents' thinking to other dinner party guests, change the spelling by deed poll and get on with your life. If you live in Australia but you're originally from Canada, so that at least twice a month someone will say, 'Do I detect a bit of a twang?', TiVo some 'Home and Away' and learn how to talk normal.

His 'Never wait more than ten minutes for anything or anyone' is harder to live by and keep your friends, so my personal favourite from the fraternal canon is this: if somebody asks you to do something and you're sort of not sure if it's a good idea — buy tickets to Cirque du Soleil, for example, or sign up for an adult education class — don't just say 'Sure! Sounds good!' because it's three months away and you can work out all the details later. You have to imagine the thing is *tonight*. If you wouldn't feel like doing it tonight, you won't in three months. You're not going to be a better, more committed person in three months. In fact, your integrity is going to take a body blow when you find yourself standing outside the Entertainment Centre scalping an A-reserve ticket to *Saltimbanco*.

So, Golden Boy offered us £20,000 for a house, and because he suggested it, buying a property in London seemed like a good idea. 'Sure!' I said. 'Sounds good!' I could work out the details later. Details like whether I wanted to be tied to London indefinitely, unable to pick up and go if I didn't like it after all. I was pretty sure that by the time we found a house I'd be a better, more committed person anyway. I'd spent 16 years under the same roof as Golden Boy, longing to be the kind of person who made the same calibre of decisions as he did (damn it, *save your Easter eggs, DAMN IT*) so I went for it. I took the money. As previously demonstrated via the 'Bump! Cute!' debacle, I'm not a planner. I don't comparison shop; I don't ask around; I just do stuff. It's a more intuitive, bridge-burning style of decision making and although Golden Boy's life-changing offer was sensibly hedged by the idiot-proofness of property buying, I still managed to turn the whole thing to shite within a calendar month.

After just a few weeks in London, when I still didn't know Tower Bridge from the Topshop at Oxford Circus, and the briefest of searches, we found a flat in West Kensington and bought it. It was the second one we looked at and Golden Boy's house was just around the corner. Sounds good! I figured it must be a knockout neighbourhood on the cusp of gentrification if he'd decided to buy there. He probably researched it thoroughly, so I decided not to. Plus, it had 'Kensington' in the title, like Kensington Gardens and Kensington Palace. How could it not be amazing?

As it turns out, there is a little bit of a world between proper, nice Kensington (Range Rovers, housewives walking chocolate labs) and West Kensington (cars on bricks, housewives running meth labs). Anywhere in London, beautiful can be just around the corner from awful. Flat 4, 39 Charleville Road turned out to be the awful just around the corner from even worse: North End Road, a stretch of mostly boarded-up shopfronts, all-night convenience stores and off-brand chicken shops with names designed to put you in mind of, while undercutting the price and quality of, Kentucky Fried Chicken. Kensey Fried Chicken, Kentucky Frying Cottage, CFK. Most of the people who walked up and down North End Road during the day had been classed 'community ready' by social services in the very recent past and didn't feel that the absence of a companion was any reason not to hold a spirited conversation while out walking.

It didn't matter so much when I was at work all day, only running the pigeon-faeces/chicken-bone/homeless-person obstacle course down North End Road twice a day to get to and from the Tube station. Once I had no place I needed to be and an infant making her first forays into the outside world, it was hard not to notice how rough West Kensington was around the edges and right through the middle. I don't know what the opposite of gentrification is but over the five years we spent there, North End Road became rapidly more prole-ified. The attempted organic butcher reverted to a kebab shop; the slated artisanal bakery never got further than rustic-looking signage. Even the Poundstretcher started revising its price point.

The only other women at home with children in the neighbourhood were clusters of teen mothers who lived on the towering council estates and rocked what I know now is called 'pram face', a very, very tight high ponytail with crunchy, product-laden tendrils and a glued-down fringe, multiple gold hoop earrings in each ear (mother and baby) and puffy track pants with tapered ankles. It was just them and me at the Early Childhood Clinic, which crouched on the ground floor of a council housing block on the other side of the Talgarth Road. I don't know what anti-climb paint is, but signs bolted to the building proudly announced that the entire estate had been coated with it. Minky and I had an appointment there on the first day we were alone together after Shab went back to work. As I slalomed the stroller through a series of police signs appealing for witnesses and breathed through my mouth past three different chickenieres, each unfortunate piece of street furniture and low-end retail emporium pressed the bruise that was my poor judgement in property. The teen mothers who should have been forced further west by the time my more advantaged offspring was born were already in the waiting room standing in line to get bike locks when Minky and I struggled through the door. I wasn't sure, that first visit, what the bike locks were for until the receptionist pointed a lacquered fingernail at the sign tacked up to her Plexiglas booth, right next to the one about how staff have a right not to be assaulted. If you don't want to be assaulted, logic says don't give your clients a heavy metal chain and make them wait 50 minutes in a hot room full of crying babies. The bike lock, as it happened, was to chain up your stroller while you saw the nurse.

It's the only baby clinic I've ever been to that employed a kind of triage system. The babies dressed in the most age-inappropriate ensemble (a mini cheerleader onesie, a studded denim jacket so rigid the newborn couldn't bring its arms down) were taken in first, followed by those whose formula had been made up using flat Pepsi Max. There was a separate queue for newborns whose bebe-studs had become infected. When I made it to the front of the line, the Jamaican midwife was pleased to discover that I already knew you don't try and make a newborn take a bottle by letting it lick a Dorito first to 'get more thirsty'. Not only that, I was breast-feeding and my baby daddy didn't think my doing so was well minging, innit. She ticked my name off a dot-matrix print-out and slid my notes back over her desk — 'I don't need to weigh no bebe with a chin roll' — together with another fistful of pamphlets, this time on birth control and polytechnics with childcare facilities. Bike lock off, we were done. It was a strange, lonely appointment. I missed my mother. I missed feeling at home. I felt simultaneously like a rich white cow *and* a lower-middle-class waster whose bad choices meant my baby wasn't getting seen to in a nice clinic, with nice mothers who chose nice non-made-up baby names and spelled them the normal way.

It didn't help that in neighbourhoods like West Kensington, official literature provided by the NHS couldn't afford to make any assumptions about your parenting. The health department copywriters had clearly been instructed to strike a tone that was upbeat and nonjudgemental but sufficiently direct to head off a whole world of ill-informed mothering. A leaflet called 'Let's Not Shake Our Babies!' sat alongside another headed 'Drugs and Co-Sleeping Are Less Than Ideal!' in a wire rack bolted to the wall of the waiting room. I picked out 'Babies Like Eye Contact!' and from it I learned it was good to occasionally look directly at your baby. Apparently a child learns to communicate this way and not by watching 'The Weakest Link' in a Jumperoo or listening to its parents fight over benefit payments in the next room. There was no pamphlet on feeling horribly lonely, though. Nothing with an eye-catching title like 'How to Carve up the Foreseeable Future with Your Small Child into Manageable Chunks Despite Your Lack of Mummy Friends, Direction, Purpose, Help or Money!' and some clip art of a mother with big cartoony tears rolling down her face onto an empty diary page. Outside of the clinic, I didn't even have the teen mothers for company. Put off by my advanced years, they stuck to themselves. They had other things to do anyway, like fighting in the street and getting pregnant again. The only neighbours who were drawn to me at all were those with less valid reasons than teen parenthood to be at a loose end in the middle of the day, the time when normal, successful people are at their most required.

Maybe I have an inviting face, or maybe the mentally disturbed could smell my quiet longing for company the way unleashed dachshunds can smell denuded chicken drumsticks in communal rubbish bins. Eventually I would learn to walk with my head downcast and avoid any eye contact with the crazy people, but as I pushed the stroller home from the clinic, a youngish man in black jeans and a parachute jacket, sporting one of those vicious-looking haircuts you mostly see in Eastern Europe, came around the corner and began walking towards me. He seemed to be staring at the air just above me. As he got closer, I looked past him, praying under my breath that he would keep going, please keep going, please don't stop. Nope, he was stopping. His wonky, bloodshot eyes only made it look like he hadn't seen me, when actually he'd been staring at me for the last 50 metres.

'You need baby-sitter?' he asked, leaning into Minky's stroller and running his zipper slowly up and down its tracks. 'I am childcare verker.'

'Yep, no, I'm fine thanks,' I said, reaching down to put a hand over Minky.

'Your friend, they need baby-sitter?' I was scared, but not scared enough that his assumption about my supposed social position ('Girls, I found a great baby-sitter!') didn't smart a little bit. The mentalist didn't know that the adventure in mummy-friend making hadn't begun for me yet and that, right at that moment, I wasn't heavy on daytime pals.

'Yep, no, we're all fine,' I insisted, while trying to drag the stroller backwards up my front steps. I couldn't decide if he was just being proactive about finding a job — perhaps approaching strangers in the street is the way people arrange childcare in Europe's less developed nations — or whether he was an undercover officer with child services. If I answered, 'Yes! I do need baby-sitter! I'm literally *dying* for some me-time,' while handing over my baby and my house keys, he might have pulled an ID badge out from inside his grubby track-suit jacket and reported me. Even in the midst of dealing with a possible white slave trader, I summoned the street smarts to knock on my own front door and wait outside until he passed. That way he wouldn't know where I lived and come back later to redouble his offer of home help. He moved on; I unlocked the door and went inside. Minky and I looked around for a minute, as though both freshly startled that this really was it, our home for the time being, our perch.

I had done my best with it. I kept the kitchen floor mopped, stored our CDs out of view and would not let Shab house a wine rack in the empty fireplace even though, as he reminded me often, it fitted perfectly. Seriously, like a *glove*. I had also figured out that, whereas poor people tend to push their furniture back against the wall and own too many couches, rich people usually own fewer sofas than they could justify and arrange them in centralised clusters to create separate seating zones. I made sure that no furniture ever touched the wall, as a kind of desperate class signifier. The flat was nice according to other people, but I had spent so much time there feeling extremely average, I couldn't see it. My decorating style — while limited by budget and the fact that until a few weeks before I had to get to and from Ikea by Tube — was based on one precept, a visceral, aching need to preserve my mental health, which meant: no mess, no junk, no plastic bags rolled up and shoved in the fruit bowl with keys, phone and two pears on the turn. No framed prints of Van Gogh's *Sunflowers* or that couple dancing under umbrellas on, I want to say, a train platform but it could be a windy beach. No shoes by the front door, no visible cables, no handbags or jackets slung over the sofa in a grim little tangle. To create solace, calm and respite from the endless confrontation that was London hammering on the front door, it had to be plain and neat and as serene as a flat can be when upstairs has a wet cough.

Above the marble fireplace at one end of the living room was an oversize mirror, and floor-to-ceiling bookcases on each side, which Shab and Golden Boy had built, neatly stacked with books. We had a comfortable, soft sofa and dark grey carpet we had put down to replace the rotty sisal that was staple-gunned to the floor in non-matching squares when we moved in. We had renovated the small, windowless kitchen, starting the day after two lines came up on my wee stick, and in the process discovered a large hole in the floor under the sink that was letting the best part of the smoke and noise upstairs. We filled it in and made 200 return trips to the Brent Cross Ikea on the Bakerloo line, eventually bringing home an entire Faktum kitchen, piece by piece. The flat had one bedroom, and Minky's crib was slotted into the corner between our bed and the window. When I realised how many hours I would spend at home, folding washing or walking lengths of the living room to try and calm Minky, we replaced the blinds that covered the three giant sash windows facing the street with shutters, so that I could see out and the lady with the wig and drawn-on eyebrows who lived opposite us and spent her mornings standing on the footpath outside our house trying to look in, knocking on the glass occasionally to gauge my thoughts re lending her money, could not.

There was nothing more to do with it, and nothing I could do about it. This was home base for the foreseeable future, so all I could do was work out how to live here with a child and not sink back under the crazy water. I couldn't now. The stakes were too high. I would be ruining somebody's actual life, not just being a bit lackadaisical with my own and super annoying to my husband. One day, I would be out of here, I told myself every morning as I sidestepped a fresh heap of turdlettes on my way to the car. One day, I would have a real house, full of friends. Family nearby, scary people far away in purpose-built facilities. I would have someone else to clean my bath, a trampoline with sides and piles of brightly coloured gumboots on the veranda. All I had to do was stay sane until that time came. Figuring out how exactly would take many more houses, an international move, six more years — oh, and, you know, $800,000, but that part wasn't my business. That part was Shab's own private nightmare. My goal at that exact moment was not crying, before lunch.

5

DAY IN, DAY OUT

THEY NEEDN'T TEACH EXPECTANT MOTHERS HOW TO DO UP A
Huggie or recognise the perfect latch when breast-feeding.
Eventually we will work those things out, even if it involves
a lot of swearing and spilt fluids to begin with. The only thing
the National Childbirth Trust ought to run classes on is how to
manage a big, long, empty day with a mewling neonate.

Maternity leave was the first time in my entire life that I'd
been mistress of my own time. School, university, work — I was
never truly off the grid then. I always had somewhere to be, at
a certain time, wearing a particular thing. Once at-home-hood
began, nobody was wondering where I was or what I was up
to at any time of day, week in, week out, week in, week out,
week in, week out … OK, stop. It felt weird. It felt bad, actually.

It was a strange, jangly sort of realisation that if I didn't plan anything, nothing would happen. If I didn't go out for 14 consecutive days, nobody except, please Jesus, my husband would notice or call to find out what I'd been up to. Having a baby sent me off the edge of society's radar and it was up to me to work out whether that was going to be lovely or a total free fall.

Every day began the same way. With a click. The Click. The sound of Shab pulling the door closed behind him and leaving Minky and me to it. After a week, I started to dread the moment of that click. I would surreptitiously watch him chase the last milky spoonful of cereal around the bowl, with a rising sense that I may at any minute start screaming like the shut-in from *Jane Eyre*. Invariably the moment would come, and I would take a deep breath, smile bravely at Minky propped up on the sofa and say, 'Soooo ... what are you in the mood for, then?' as if we were new acquaintances on a blind date that wouldn't end. 'Do you feel like reading or ... shall we eat something? Or we could just look out the window for a bit?'

And now an amendment, vis-à-vis managing a day being the only thing new mothers have to learn. That is not true at all. There are about a million things to learn, from the concrete (car seat buckles, removing Sudocrem from various fabric types, how to do up press studs in the dark) to the abstract (time management, healthy self-talk and, later, lying to toddlers). There was a bunch of practical stuff I didn't know that, looking back, might have been helpful. For instance, whether you are allowed to leave the baby on its own in a room and go into another room. I assumed you weren't, so I carried Minky around the house with me at all times, like a Fendi Peakaboo bag in a rough bar. If she came with a strap, I would have wound it around my wrist. When occasionally I had the good fortune of getting her to sleep on my bed (since I also thought the crib was only for night-time) I dragged a cushion, some food and something to read into my room and sat on the floor beside her until she woke up. Then I would carry her into the bathroom with me and finally do the wee I'd been hanging on to for 45 minutes while she snoozed. Now I would walk to the shops and leave a newborn sleeping at home if I thought I could get away with it, but back then, I capped out at four feet.

Actually, that's not true either, about me running to the shops and leaving a child behind. I tried it once and the gods of high-risk parenting punished me with the full force of their fury. Minky was five and Bitsy, who comes later, was two. It was a hot, wet day and the house we lived in then had a corner store out and across the back lane. I had no roads to cross, I didn't have to get in the car, and the children were so flopsy and relaxed watching 'Play School' in their underpants that their mouths had fallen open. I had a little menstrual situation (I mention this only so you know I was taking care of urgent lady business, not going on an unnecessary magazine run). Instead of interrupting the children, coaxing them into clothes, finding shoes and carrying Bitsy to the shop in the rain while Minky accidentally stabbed me in the face over and over with her 'Charlie and Lola' umbrella, I decided it would be OK to leave Minky in charge, run over and be back with some feminine requisites literally five minutes later. The house was quiet, safe and child-proofed, and I took my phone, which Minky knew how to call. I was gone less than five minutes but when I opened the secure back gate I heard bone-melting screams coming from the house. I dropped the packet of supremely price-inflated Libras (at that particular corner store one sanitary pad works out to, like, $14) and ran into the house to find that a large black bird had flown in through the window during my impossibly brief absence. The bird was stressed, flapping, knocking into the windows and panic-defecating all over the house, while the girls stood in the hallway in their underpants going like this: 'Aaaaaaaaaaaaaaaaaaaaaaaaaaaa aaaaaaagh', eyes shut and arms waving above their heads.

So, back to when I didn't leave Minky ever. I also didn't know how often you were supposed to bathe a newborn, or how soon after birth you were supposed to *start* bathing one. Because we were ejected from hospital before Minky was given her first bath, I just didn't think about it until she was three weeks old and starting to smell a little high. Whose baby still had vernix in the folds under her arms at nearly a month old? Mine! There should be some kind of prize for that, other than the smell of her cheesy neck folds, which many would say is prize enough. Later on, when I was trying to establish a kind of evening routine to combat the demented crying fit with which Minky liked to round out each day, I didn't know if you were meant to do dinner then bath, or bath first then dinner. I had no-one to ask, since the problem of time zones meant I couldn't call my mother or mother-in-law the minute I hit a gap in my know-how. I had to save up my questions for an appropriately timed once-a-weeker, which made it doubly frustrating when either would say, after a spell of silent thinking, 'To be honest, I don't really remember. It was all so *different* when we did it.' Apparently one generation back, mothers didn't bathe their children in water, feed them food or dress them in clothes — it was all *so* different. Instead of waiting around for that, I'd guess, and usually wrong. Feed a clean, shampooed, be-suited baby some mashed spinach and see if you don't have to start all over again at ten past eight.

I was clueless at a lot of the practical stuff, but there was one thing I quickly learned to be totally, winningly, unfailingly superb at without taking any kind of class and it was not how to remove guano from plush carpet with a maxi pad. It was the art of rallying. Rallying is an indispensable, fundamental survival skill for the currently-at-home. Veterans will have pulled off half a dozen dazzling rallies before morning tea, but for the newcomers, this is what rallying looks like:

It is a Tuesday, the most innately rally-requiring day of the week. I wake up feeling flat and tired, and my hair is greasy. I have no plans for the day, and there is half a pot of expired ricotta in the fridge and nothing else. My impulse is to sink back into bed and find somebody other than myself to be mad at about this dismal vignette. But with a baby to care for, I cannot waste time apportioning blame to the absent. The success of the day is all me. So I get up; I take a freaking shower. I rally. I eat cereal with some slightly sharp ricotta, while packing a bag for the day. The baby goes down for a sleep while I vacuum the living room, which serves the dual purpose of sucking up dirt and blocking out the sound of crying, mine and hers. I open a window, let a breeze in and look forward to getting a takeaway coffee. I rally. There is nothing else I can do. Even if, beforehand, I'm all 'Oh, but I don't feel like it.' I will *never* feel like it. Of course I won't feel like it. If I feel like it, it's not rallying, it's just being happy. Rallying will always take every scrap of self-discipline a person has, but the alternative is so much worse.

The alternative is staying in my sleepwear until mid-morning and thinking hateful thoughts about the curtains. The baby has half a feed, then half a sleep, which is one whole lot of useless, while I let myself get so hungry that even opening the mail seems overwhelming. I try to get one more day out of my last hair wash than it can happily give me, so that all day I feel scratchy around the hairline. When I finally get to the park, all the women who rallied sooner than I did are leaving. So I go home and, smackdown, turn the television on or read the kind of celebrity gossip websites that make me feel dirty afterwards. I gave up, I didn't rally, and now I am a sloppy, greasy, hungry stay-at-homer who has run out of topics at 11.14 a.m., when it's still ten hours until I can legitimately go to bed.

I spent most of my childhood in a small New Zealand university town on an eerie tableland between two mountain ranges. There was only one kind of weather there, a gusty, glary, overcast fug that my mother called Tight Hat Weather. It gave you a permanent low-grade headache like you were wearing a too-small beanie. And someone else's prescription glasses. On a long coach ride, after half-swallowing a fish-oil capsule that keeps repeating on you, and for no reason your fingers smell powerfully of orange. To opt for not-rallying was to let loose a Tight Hat weather system in my own house. I would feel cranky and worthless and sick. I would start fantasising about going back to work. Strange, despicable thoughts like 'I could put my baby in the boot and drive to the ocean' would float into my mind involuntarily, causing me to wonder if I was already unhinged. Sometimes, if I skated near the edge for too long, skimmed a little too much eonline.com, I would have to break what felt like an impossible rally into bite-sized pieces, as small and manageable as the peeled, quartered grapes that really choke-phobic mothers cart around in microscopic Tupperwares.

The first step in a bite-sized rally is always: have a shower. Once you're a mother, pregnant ladies ask you for advice all the time, without even checking first that you're any good at it. Just by dint of doing it before them, you get to be an authority. The only thing I can ever think to offer an expectant mother is: have a shower. 'In fact,' I'll say, 'it's a good idea to have a shower before your husband leaves.' And then, because she looks sad and confused, I'll add, 'Leaves in the morning, I mean. Not *leaves* leaves.'

I figured out early on that Shab would have a much more robust perception of my coping if he didn't farewell his wife each morning in the exact same gamey T-shirt and sweat pants she was wearing the previous evening and would be wearing again, for his visual feasting, later that night. The last thing a new mother needs is a nervy, hyper-vigilant life partner who keeps threatening to take her to the GP for a depression questionnaire, just because of lazy dressing. Those tests need to be rewritten for mothers anyway. I've done a hundred of them, and while the emotions they describe might be red flags in normal society, any woman with children will have cycled through most of them before ABC Kids goes off at 10 a.m. Do I feel like crying seldom, sometimes, frequently, all of the time? I have children, a-hole. I feel like crying all of the time. Why would you even ask me that?

Even better than rallying is arranging daily life such that I wouldn't have anything to rally from, no hidden troughs of unscheduled time to fall into and then claw my way out of. That is intermediate-level day management, though, and I had to live out the full horror of a completely empty week before I would learn to start putting some shit in my diary. Not long after Shab went back to work and I emerged from the milky, snoozy bubble of immediate postpartumhood, which defies any kind of scheduling — you are just as likely to find yourself pacing the living room and eating reheated korma at 3.00 a.m. as you are at noon in those first few weeks — I decided to conduct a little experiment. I tried doing nothing. Guess what happened? Nothing. The phone didn't ring; the front door didn't open to a nice, friendly friend holding two takeaway coffees and a stack of recent *Vogues*. The contents of the fridge dwindled to nothing and Minky got more and more irritable, while I got more and more irritated at her. Doing nothing wasn't going to work. It took maybe three days of nothing to work that out.

So, what did we actually do all day? Gosh, I *hate* that question. Even now, after so many years at home, it still makes me bristle. Even when it's me asking me, and not a hot woman at Shab's work Christmas party who still has a job and self-esteem. The question rarely comes from men, actually. Men seem resigned to the fact that all women, working or not, spend their days doing slightly mysterious, unfathomable things. It is really only women who ask it, with their emphasis usually on the second *do*. What do you *do* all day?

When the question was new to me, in that first spell at home, it struck me as strange rather than inherently judgemental. You would think the baby strapped to my front would have tipped everyone off. 'I "do" that,' I would say, pointing. 'I wipe it, I read to it, I feed it, I rock it, I change it, and now I even bathe it.' So much of what I did all day, I concede, was invisible. When Shab left in the morning the square foot of floor under the highchair was clean, and when he came home it was also clean. Nothing had changed, but only because I had been down there on my hands and knees four times since breakfast with a Pine O Cleen Wipe. Although I can so vividly see the contents of that balled-up wipe in my mind's eye (two pasta shells, some sand, a regurgitated blueberry and a hair), no-one could see the effort it took to make sure everything stayed exactly the same. At the end of every day, I would still make Shab tour the house like Prince Philip, hands clasped behind his back, admiring my invisible labour, but it failed to gratify.

There would be no evidence either of the hours I would put in later as the advance team, security attaché and cleanup crew for my despotic little toddler president — thrusting a hand around a sharp table corner just as a soft forehead careened towards it, throwing myself bodily between a flying NERF ball and a glass vase, diving across the end of a too-slippery slippery dip. Second by second, preventing, watching, cushioning and monitoring so

76

the house and the child remained unbroken. Indispensable, yet completely invisible until the second I stopped doing it.

If ever I attempted to outline the events of an entire day, point by point, the answer would stultify the listener and depress the narrator: 'Well,' I would say, looking heavenward for inspiration, 'today I made Bolognese at nine a.m., with mince that wasn't totally unfrozen. I checked my email, then I ate some mandarin. Oh, and I got a package!' It's not the answer they're looking for. They are fishing for a more philosophical answer to the implied questions 'How do you bear it?' and 'How can you justify it?', so I never gave it then and still don't. 'Mostly,' I'd rather say, 'I spend my days avoiding anyone who might ask me that.' Because neither could I capture, even if I wanted to, a day's high points, although they were many and both reason and reward for all the hard work. Sometimes, for example, Minky and I would go back to bed after Shab left. I would feed her in bed and then we would fall asleep together in a warm, blankety muddle. I would be woken by a little sniffle or her tiny hand on my face. We would lie there for a bit longer, her eyes locked on me as I talked about nothing, and it would be magic — but I wouldn't be able to describe it later. 'We had this lovely bit of eye contact,' I would try and tell Shab at day's end, 'and I don't know, it was like — well, it was lovely, but I can't really ...'

And so the question kept coming, and it remains: what *did* I do all day? Especially when I didn't have a home to make, homemaker style; a mother to visit; or, as yet, that many friends with children I could arrange to hook up with. To begin with, when Minky was happy to spend protracted periods in her stroller and I was yet to wear out my welcome with myself, we just freestyled it. We went out. A lot. We took long walks through Notting Hill. We went to cafés and bookshops, and a million times to Kensington Gardens and Hyde Park, regardless of the temperature. I learned to breast-feed in cafés without showing any nip, and only once did I spray another patron's overcoat with breast milk, because I was still learning that, contrary to popular belief, milk does not issue from a person's bosom in a single stream as though from a child's water pistol, but in many separate directions and with mixed force, as though from a shower head at a rented holiday house. I mind-mapped all the shops and municipal buildings in the Royal Borough of Kensington and Chelsea with clean baby-change facilities. As we got through winter and it started to warm up again, we spent more and more time in the park or just walking through nice parts of London and pretending I wasn't sore-footed or lonely.

Often our outings would be pegged on some kind of errand. These were almost always made up, and had I had something more fun to do, they could have waited. 'Buy stamps' or 'Get some of those felt circles to go under chair legs' I'd write on a blank diary page. Sometimes, when I had been out the previous day and purchased all the batteries and light bulbs our cupboards could hold, the brief would be even looser, like 'Go to the hardware and buy something that costs less than £3' or just 'Go out. Don't cry.' If we could get distracted, or stop for coffee, or find some grass or a library, we'd stay out longer. Only fatigue, a serious code brown or running out of parking money would send us home.

When I say I had no friends, that isn't strictly true. I had the Snooch to begin with, and lots of other pre-baby chums, but they were at work all day. I lacked reliable daytime company. Other women I had come into contact with and might have tried to spend more time with had much older children and were so embedded in the world of motherhood already that I felt like a blundering intruder whenever Minky and I visited at a time of day when a clued-up mother would know you never visit — nap time, arsenic hour, the weekend. The same mothers would stare incredulously when I'd mention how we'd just done two whole feed-wake-sleep cycles on the King's Road (excellent change facilities, first floor, Peter Jones) instead of feeding at home, going out for 35 minutes of fresh air, then hurrying back to base for the next cot-based self-settle and sleep like a good, normal mother would. Lizzie was the head mother in this circle. Her efficiency and togetherness had been intimidating before I had children, but afterwards, I traded my ill-informed judgement for a celebrity/celebrity's-biggest-fan kind of awe. I wanted to be near her as much as possible, just watching.

Because her oldest child is two years older than Minky, Lizzie now seemed to me as though she had parenting wrapped up, even if secretly she was winging it like everybody else. She had her second baby a couple of weeks after Minky was born and already had a proper house with that converted loft, as well as two separate living areas and the right ratio of bedrooms to family members. She had piles of purpose-built baby equipment (her blonde-wood change table was my towel on the bed) and her babies all slept and ate beautifully. Even though we live on opposite sides of the world now, I still consult Lizzie about important parenting questions, like a) when to introduce nut products into your child's diet, b) how much pocket money is appropriate and c) whether those mothers who you only ever see in gym gear actually are on their way to/from the gym.*

It was Lizzie who, in the gentlest way, suggested that staying out for hours at a time was a bit peculiar and not really that fair on Minky, especially as she got older. Our eight-hour outings in a noisy, crowded city might also explain why the poor over-stimulated child couldn't wind down at night except by screaming herself to total exhaustion and taking me down with her, so that Shab would often come home at night to find the two of us passed out wherever we had finally fallen. After a few months, the outings were starting to lose some of their

---

* a) consult your GP, b) one unit of currency per year of age, c) no they are not.

original gloss for me too. Bearing in mind I'd given birth not so long ago, was awake for great swathes of the night-time and was breast-feeding like a battery cow, I was usually knackered before we left the house and skyrockets-delirious by the time we got home.

There are women who go the other way, apparently, in this phase of life — who let themselves become so overwhelmed by the prospect of going out with a baby, from packing the bag to finding a car space at the other end, that they end up rooted in their own living rooms. Overnight they turn into voluntary agoraphobics whose husbands have to open the curtains when they come home at night. The other day I called a friend with a newborn to see if she'd like to come over for afternoon tea. 'Look, I'd *like* to, but I just can't,' she said. 'By the time I get there and get home and everything, it won't be worth it. But,' she added without any kind of irony, 'in two years I totally could.' I could smell the drawn drapes from down the phone.

Back then, I almost always overreached with my outings. I thought I could do an entire morning at the Tate Modern with a newborn, then Selfridges, the library and a Sainsbury's, when, of course, I couldn't without feeling loose-legged with fatigue by early afternoon. I would find myself suddenly too far afield — Primrose Hill, say, or Hampstead — and all I would want was to close my eyes and be home, but I knew it would be an hour before I feasibly could be. I always underestimated how long it would take to get home and attempt to make it before Minky's next feed, so that if we got tied down in traffic or missed a bus she would howl with hunger and I would have to find somewhere to sit and feed her. I breast-fed hundreds of times pulled over in the car, with her in the front seat on my lap, trying to manage the angles and elbows and flow of liquid — which, word, does not come out of car upholstery. I fed at bus stops, in the changing rooms at House of Fraser, in the back office of an Office shoe store, and more times than I could count on a park bench, which in London in February is playing it fast and loose with frostbite of the breastal region.

'You might want to start thinking about spending a bit more time at home and getting her into a proper routine,' Lizzie suggested one day as I sat at her kitchen table, watching her chop up fruit so quickly and skilfully that the knife looked blurry. 'Children need routine and she isn't a newborn who can just go anywhere any more.'

'But at least she is a faaaaabulous eater,' I said, as I fed five-month-old Minky some of the stoned and peeled peach that Lizzie's daughter had just rejected. I had just been called out on my rubbish baby day management so I changed the subject to food, because I was pretty sure I was nailing food.

Every mother needs something she can feel superior about, whether it's that her baby slept through the night from 20 minutes old, or that her child hasn't slept through once ('You don't know tired until …'). A mother may choose to boast that she has more help than everyone else she knows, or none at all; that her child is the most social being you'll ever meet, or a fierce and demanding cling-on who will be held by no-one else. Whatever combination of habits and preferences fate happened to throw at her baby, chances are one of them can be moulded into the perfect rod for beating other mothers whose babies were dealt a different set of qualities.

I chose food. Ever since Minky was born I'd been looking around for something to be awe-inspiring at. It really was short rations in that department. I tried a couple of times being all 'Get me, I'm raising our baby in a one-bedroom flat!' but that tended to generate tsks of pity rather than the quiet self-reproach that I was looking to inspire in my house-owning listeners. When I tried to flaunt my youth in front of the 40-year-old first-time mothers I met at Lizzie's, they would look at Minky like she'd been conceived on formal night after eight Bacardi Breezers. My husband's earning power wasn't an option either — the mothers from nearby Fulham had already bagsed that particular USP — nor was he the most incompetent father any woman had ever had to co-parent with, another popular option, definitely. Minky was an average sleeper — not good, not bad — and my mother-in-law is not The Most Irritating Woman in the World, so that was out. Besides, I'd already met a woman who was working the mother-in-law angle to unbeatable effect. Her mother-in-law got so nervous about feeding her grown-up children and their partners for Sunday lunch — timing the vegetables to finish just as the meat came out, that kind of thing — that instead of making anything on the day, she'd cook an entire roast dinner (peas, boiled carrots, roast potatoes, two chickens, everything) three days early. She'd plate up ten individual servings, right down to a puddle of gravy and some stuffing, GLAD Wrap each plate and stack them in her freezer. Then, when the company arrived, all she needed to do was microwave the plates one by one. 'I've got quite a big one coming next. Who would like a big one? One of the boys?' she'd call out from the kitchen. How defrosting and rewarming ten freezer-burned dinners one after the other was easier than waiting five minutes for the peas, I don't know, but I do know that with ineptitude like that in the world, there was no way my maternal calling card could be mother-in-law related.

It would have to be food. Minky's *amazing* dietary preferences and my even more *amazing* dedication to her broad and sophisticated palate would be my little bit of in-your-face-ness. To make sure, I spent most of my at-home time husking quinoa, steaming organic papaya and sourcing quality non-GM millet to make porridge. I bought books on infant nutrition; I made appointments with dieticians; I scoured the VegSoc website for information on whether a vegetarian diet is safe for babies and learned that it is as long as your child will tolerate a teaspoon of iron-rich molasses at every meal time, which my *amazing* baby did. I may have been failing Minky in half a dozen significant ways but in dietary terms this child was the chosen one. I even made up her vegetable purées with breast milk (mini-sick!) and, in fact, liquids wise, she drank nothing that hadn't come out of my bosoms or a water purifier until she was two. She snacked on slices of raw silken tofu, and she had definitely never, ever eaten jar food.

If you were any kind of earthy parent in 2004, you were deeply disdainful of jar food. The banana custard laced with dextrose, the lamb casserole in smoothie form. This was before those little squishy-sided packets of only-vegetable purées had been invented, instantly destigmatising factory-made baby food and creating an entire generation of toddlers who stumble around the park self-administering pumpkin and sweet corn at ten in the morning. There would be no jar food for Minky, and I would lord that over anybody foolish enough to ask me what I was feeding her, while they shook up a jar of Stage One Hearty Beef for their own unfortunate spawn. I can still deliver most of the painfully self-righteous explanation of her favourite meal's ingredients, its preparation, origin and benefits to a developing neural system, only now I have to be three champagnes in.

One day, though, the day before we were flying out of London for a week with Shab's parents, I'd kind of had to run down the fridge. We were all out of sheep's-milk cheese and home-made polenta rusks. I would have to feed Minky store-bought food for 24 hours, until I could get off the plane in New York and start reconstituting some sulphate-free Turkish apricots. I felt so guilty and embarrassed even paying for it that I padded out the purchase with tampons, home-brand condoms and a bumper pack of Canesten pessaries — anything to draw the cashier's eye away from my squalid, incriminating purchase of a half-dozen pots of Holle organic pumpkin.

Minky and I happened to be on the Fulham Road, near a Caffè Nero, with the brown paper bag that might as well have held a Fisher-Price My First Crack Pipe. The Nero was big enough to accommodate the stroller, and because it meant another 30 minutes out of the house, I decided we would stop in for a large latte and some jar poison. I ordered my coffee, sat down and popped the lid off one of the toxic varietals. Minky expressed no visible emotion. I wrapped my fingers around the jar to hide the label and dipped a spoon in. As I coaxed the first spoonful into Minky's formerly unsullied mouth, guaranteeing her a lifetime of obesity and oppositional defiant disorder, the door behind me swung open and a man in a navy pullover and expensive-looking trousers walked in. A few minutes later, he sat down next to me and placed a roast-vegetable panini and a perfectly folded newspaper on the table.

I looked up without thinking, holding aloft the spoon loaded with artificial thickener, and saw that the man was Hugh

Grant. Hugh Grant and his panini at the table beside me! And there was me with jar food! Can you imagine how much that then-childless male actor must have been judging me? I know it looked like he was ignoring us completely and reading his paper but he was so not. Hugh Grant was pretending to read while mentally denigrating a mother who didn't love her own baby enough to mash a fricking banana. I had to do something before he went home with the wrong idea about me or texted Liz Hurley. So I did what every mother does when she needs to communicate a difficult or pressing truth to an adult nearby who cannot, for whatever reason, be spoken to directly. I talked theatrically to my baby.

'Ooh, Minky, isn't this funny food? This isn't like Mummy's yummy food, is it? You've never HAD THIS BEFORE, HAVE YOU MINKY, but we're GOING OVERSEAS TOMORROW, aren't we, sweet pea? And Mummy had to RUN DOWN THE FRIDGE.' Hugh Grant never looked up from his paper. Still, I am sure he heard me and repented of his hasty misconceptions.

The Nero date was a typical time killer for Minky and me — coffee after some errands — but Lizzie was right. Minky was getting too big to be out for hours and sleep wherever she could. Plus it was getting harder and harder to think of things to do. The alternative though — hours and hours and hours inside — was frightening.

And then Spackers called. We should chat, she said, about whether I wanted to come back to *The Times* a few days a week, or full time. That she wanted me back was flattering; that they could offer me something part time was intriguing. The money would be nice, and more and more I was thinking, why go and do errands when I could just lie on the floor and look at the lights until spots came in front of my eyes? If I took my job back, I could call time on this endless loop of mashed swede, dirty bibs, *Goodnight Moon* and scrabbling around for coins to feed the insatiable parking meters outside Holland Park. I could leave behind this exhausting invention of a day's weft and sail back into the gratifying, socially valued world of work and the higher calling that is Writing Lifestyle Features. I would know what I did all day. I could answer that question, and the one that follows it as surely as a toddler follows its mother into the bathroom. 'And do you work or ...?'

6

AND DO YOU WORK OR ...?

EVERYBODY NEEDS A THING. EVEN THOUGH LOOKING AFTER Minky was the hardest thing I'd ever done, it didn't qualify as an actual *thing*. 'I mean, don't get me wrong,' says Nessa, from 'Gavin & Stacey', about her infant son. 'I loves Neil the Baby. He's a good bloke. But at the end of the day, he's needy. He's always after something.' Minky was a conveyer belt of need, but just meeting each one before they stacked up in an insurmountable pile didn't count as a life's calling. Work would give me a thing, that was certain. I could say I was a journalist again. My days would be set out for me and all I would have to do was show up.

While I was still pregnant, I told anyone who asked, and many who didn't, that I would go back when the baby was one, as though I could be certain that after exactly 12 months' being with her, it would cease to feel necessary and she would cease to be interesting. The baby and I would both thank each other for everything; what a great year, we'd say, and without surfeit emotion, we'd both move on. Now that she was flesh and blood — or rather, little shoes, laughter, blonde curls and red cheeks — I knew there would never be a decision made concerning her that didn't involve a surfeit of emotion.

I loved her *so* much. It is such an obvious thing to say that parents can forget to out loud. During an argument with my mother when I was 11 and cheesed that she wouldn't buy me a pleather jerkin I had my eye on — apparently it was 'tacky', as *if* — I sat on the kitchen counter chewing my hair and trying to think of the meanest thing I could say to her. 'I love Dad more than I love you' didn't do it. She just shrugged when I told her she 'smelled old'.

'You never tell me you love me.' That got her, especially since it wasn't true. She was incensed — how could I be so awful? Every thing she did, every bed she changed, every uniform she ironed, every breath she took was her telling me she loved me. She shouldn't need to say it with actual words as well, and still she did.

I told Minky I loved her roughly every 30 minutes, if only so that later she couldn't be intentionally vicious during a jerkin-related standoff. In those first months, when the love was new, it felt physical and compulsive. If I'd known I was allowed to leave the room she was in, I'm not sure I would have. I could stare at her for hours, in a kind of trance, like she was a campfire. Everything she did was miraculous to me — every blink, every sneeze. She would cough and I'd want to write a song. To begin with she could only respond by blowing slurpy spit bubbles in my face. Then one day, a few years later, she would stare back at me, put two dimpled hands on my face and say, 'Mummy? I love you *so* hardly.' Until then I didn't mind that the traffic was entirely one way. I loved her hardly enough for both of us.

The next time Minky and I walked past the daycare centre around the corner from our house, I slowed down and tried to imagine her inside. It was in the basement of another terrace house, with two barred windows looking up to the street. It wasn't Dickensian or anything. There was children's artwork stuck to the windows and I couldn't smell gruel or pox ointment wafting up the concrete stairs. Had it been a proper Victorian workhouse with a rat problem, or staff recruited straight from the sex offenders register, it would have been an open and shut thing, but it looked averagely fine. She probably would be fine there. If I started early enough, she wouldn't know any different. I started thinking about it.

When I say I started thinking about it, really I started arguing violently with myself like one of the nutties on North

End Road. It was a properly bipolar kind of affair. I did all the voices, although the opposing positions were based on women I knew who'd chosen one or the other. Like a good daughter, I let my own mother inform what I understood to be normal and right. Nora Ephron says if your mother told you never to buy a red coat, you'll be 40 before you do, and even then you'll wear it once and feel uncomfortable the entire time. My mother stopped working when my brother was born and spent most of my childhood lying on her bed reading fuzzy-page library copies of Thomas Hardy novels, while Golden Boy and I tried to catch eels in the rapid-flowing river that ran across the back of our sloping back lawn. Eels could be traded for 50-cent mixes at the Thwaites's Dairy on the corner, which we'd walk to at close of play, dragging the eels behind us in an old pillowcase. Mrs Thwaites was Welsh or something and made pies with them, which now seems too Roald Dahl-ish to be true, but we got free sweets, so we didn't ask questions. My brother in bare feet and stubbies, me in red clogs and a Mickey Mouse sweatshirt, my mother at home with *Jude the Obscure*. She is still on maternity leave now, even though I am her youngest child and I'm 33.

Janet Frame described her mother as being so present throughout her childhood that she has no precise memories of her. Her mother became a kind of maternal shadow, always somewhere in the background with a basket of laundered sheets needing to be hung out. In one way, that's the kind of mother I wanted to be, so present I'd be allowed to ignore my children and make them go and do stuff on their own, although not in the street with a pillowcase of eels. Benign neglect is a luxury that only mothers who are always there can afford in this precise historical moment of helicoptering, Velcro parenting, or whichever new nickname the Saturday papers have most recently applied to a mode of parenting that, in the end, means holding on to the chain of the swing for its entire arc. I didn't think I had the wherewithal for quality time, only quantity.

I had only one contemporary who had decided firmly against work and not returned after children. We went to school together and had fallen out of regular contact, but once, on a pre-Minky trip back to Australia, we had lunch. She had trained as a doctor, dressed well before children, and I respected her. She had been home with her son for two years when we met.

'So, what do you actually *do* all day?' I asked.

'Oh well, today, um, I found a chest of drawers in a council cleanup pile and I thought I might, like, do it up,' she said. I threw up in my mouth. I wasn't even pregnant yet; I was still working and I had places to be. The idea of such shameless make-work chilled me to the core. A smart, expensively educated woman had become the David Blaine of motherhood, expertly trained to survive unnatural periods in the suburbs by slowing down her brain function. Whereas my mother's extended maternity leave felt unquestionably normal, on a peer it seemed anachronistic and wasteful.

On the other hand, there was Spackers. Successful and impressive and asking me back. I had wanted to be like her ever since I met her, and I craved the imaginary medal I would pin to my own chest if I managed to become an official Working Mother. I missed adults, salaries, lunch. I can't describe how much I missed the clothes. Still, I couldn't banish the image of Spackers milking herself over the work basins, and I thought back to how often she would leave her desk to field phone calls from a flustered domestic, come in late, go home early and spend the bit in the middle talking about being torn in two. So that, or Thomas Hardy and bringing rubbish in off the street and rag-rolling it to stop from going mad.

Footnote, my school friend did paint those drawers. She also decoupaged the inside with cut-up wrapping paper and contact, then displayed the whole sloppy mess in her son's bedroom, until one morning she sat up in bed and said — I like to imagine, out loud — 'I PAINTED RUBBISH FROM THE STREET' and dragged them back to the kerb. At which point — I also like to imagine — a passing stay-at-home mother couldn't believe her good luck and loaded them into the boot of her station wagon. Sanded back, she'd think to herself, these drawers would be gorgeous.

Shab refused to come down on either side. On one hand, he said, it would be nice for Minky to have me around. On the other hand, he understood that work was fulfilling while at-home-hood was fulfilling but in a more soul-destroying way. I wished he would make the decision for me, although in the end it didn't matter what he thought. My answer came from within and it turned out to be as simple as that diagram from school of female repro-organs. Actually, the answer *was* that diagram: the two ovaries, and whatever that bit is in the middle, shaped kind of like a tree, with branches spread wide, the whole thing gouached in fleshy tones, with veins and vessels picked out in red and blue. For no reason I could articulate, I just had to stay home, because, at the very thought of leaving Minky, the whole entire diagram inside my body began to throb. My internal lady self started to clench and pound at the idea of sending my tiny person down those concrete stairs into the not-bad daycare or bumping a stroller down the steps of the Tube at 7.30 a.m. The closer I got to a mythical start date, the more I knew, in a deep, tree-trunky way, that this, being with Minky, was the only thing I was really irreplaceable at. This is where I was really needed right now, and since I wasn't exactly loving our life, it seemed extra cruel to run out on it and leave her to get on with things in a basement group home. No matter how bad I was at everything except perfectly balanced meals, being Minky's mother was the one thing only I could do better than anyone else, even on my worst day.

The Times was still coming out; the FT website was replete with summarised news. Even if I could have found someone to care for her — a nice Eastern European man with a parachute jacket and a competitive hourly rate — and gone back to work, there was nowhere except right here with her that I would be doing anything as important. Plus, work as I imagined it didn't exist any more. I told myself I missed it, but it wasn't the interviews or the editorial meetings I longed for, it was the freedom to have a job, to be single-minded about it and self-absorbed in that totally valid professional way. Now there was a Minky, there could be no more single-mindedness about anything. My mind would always be on her, so I might as well be with her.

And that was that. At-home-hood was no longer a brief segue from the main event of me and my career. Housewifery was permanently me now, my choice, and even though it was not the least bit like I'd imagined (the only highlights against a universe of lowlights being Minky herself and the fact we were working on a plan to leave London and move back to Australia), I would keep going.

I was in ropey knots about telling Spackers that I was never coming back. I didn't want to seem ungrateful or like a traitor to the sisterhood, even though I felt like both. I decided to do it in person, after writing and deleting 8,000 different email versions, which swung wildly in tone between Official Letter of Resignation and Teen Mother Diary Entry.

'I regret to inform you ...' delete delete delete.

'This is the hardest thing I've ever had to ...' delete delete.

I hoped Minky would turn on an insane crying spree in Spackers' office, inconsolable to all but me, and the job would be done for us, no explanation required. On the appointed day, I stowed Minky in the Björn and made my old commute from West Kensington to Tower Bridge at the un-commuter-ly hour of 11 a.m. I had only ever watched the clock on that trip to work out if I'd have time to read the entire *Metro* before my station, not whether I'd have time to get my breast out of my bra and feed somebody with it before journey's end.

Walking back into an office you once worked in is like returning to a high school from which you've been expelled. It is all unnervingly familiar — the same faces, the same furniture — but utterly closed to you now because of that *thing* you did. Your only course of action is to appear totally cool with that, like you regret nothing and just happened to be passing through, communicating by your manner and bearing a kind of 'What-up, losers?' I didn't have a security pass any more, so I had to be signed in by a new intern. She was breezy and confident, and as she clicked down that hallway beside me I could hear her internal monologue so clearly she might as well have been shouting it out her mouth. 'I work at *The Times*! I work at *The Times*! I work at *The Times*!' she was thinking; I knew because I used to think that too. I tried to think of something to say to her but I kept running into the past tense — 'I used to ...', 'When I worked here ...' — and I couldn't keep going. As soon as I walked in, Spackers stopped what she was doing and scooped Minky out of my arms. She held her the entire time we chatted, about feeding and routines and sleep, Spackers tossing out pearls of mothering wisdom faster than I could catch them. Eventually, I swallowed hard and told her that, although I was so grateful she'd offered, I would probably ... you know ... stay with Minky for the time being.

'Well, I'm sure we can find you the odd thing to write from home,' she said. I was so busy trying to memorise the thing she'd said just prior, about self-settling, that I didn't notice she'd gifted me another life changer, turning me into an official Freelance Journalist with one offhand remark. Wherever I went from then on, wherever I lived, however many babies I had, I would always have something I could do from home, because Spackers gave me those first commissions. Because of her, I would have income and a little shred of Something I could use to convince myself I wasn't Doing Nothing. I didn't thank her at the time, but I've thanked her in my head every time I've sat down to write a freelance story since. We said our goodbyes, and I packed Minky back into her pouch and headed back to the Tube. Baby skin has a tendency to absorb the scent of anything it touches. After 45 minutes in Spackers' arms, Minky had taken on her musky eau de toilette. Apparently, I would carry a little piece of my old boss with me wherever I went, starting now. As Minky and I ticked off the stations towards home — Blackfriars, St James, Earl's Court — I thought about the indefinite number of months or years ahead that would now pass uninterrupted, for the most part, by paid work. Since this was going to be a long-term thing, she and I together, the routine could use a little tweaking. Right now, though, I had other jobs to do.

7

SO MUCH JOBS

'KENT WENT TO THE BATHROOM AGAIN LAST NIGHT,' I HEARD A mother telling her friend at a café table next to mine. 'Soon as he walked in.' Both women had strollers drawn up at their sides and were drinking coffee while holding car keys in midair and shaking them. Minky and I were having what I had started to call 'work drinks', an every-Friday-afternoon café trip to mark another five days of side-by-side toil at Time-Killing Ltd.

'Oh?' the friend replied. She seemed to know exactly why Kent's trip to the bathroom was shocking and was eager for the latest instalment.

'So I said to him, "Kent, we have got to talk about you going to the toilet all the time."'

'How many nights is it now?' the friend asked.

'Eight nights in a row. Ever since we got back from away, he's been coming home and needing to go straight to the loo. He'll be in there for 15 minutes without a doubt,' she said, repositioning herself in her chair. 'So I said to him, "No, Kent, this has to stop. Why can't you do your turds at work? You've got eight hours."'

'Outrageous.'

'Yeah well, wait for this,' the woman said. Her friend barely could. 'Last night he's in there and Braydon followed him in. I was feeding Presley so I wasn't about to get up. Kent's like, "Babe, I don't want him in here!" And I said, "Tough, Kent!"'

'We never get to go to the toilet alone, why should *they*?' the friend enthused.

'Exactly. Anyway, it was fine in the end but I just said, "Kent, honestly, when you get home, I need you to help. You can't just sit around the whole time."'

Husbands can be *so* slow on the uptake. It's like Kent hadn't even worked out that post-children, adult bowels cannot be voided on an as-needed basis. The days of going to the bathroom just because you 'have to' are over, subsumed by the more pressing need to sort the recycling, BPAY for term 3 of Humpty Squad and read *The Lorax* with all the voices while mentally fasting your large intestine. When that's done, then and only then, may you take some time in the WC.

Shab didn't get it to begin with. He did wildly selfish things like walk on wooden floors with shoes on or let his mobile phone *ring* after I'd just finished patting Minky to sleep through the crib bars while my lumbar spine fused together at 90 degrees. And this one time? He came home from work and — wait for this — said he was 'a bit whacked'. I think he even did a stretch of some kind to underscore his point.

'Whacked from what?' I asked, genuinely unable to comprehend how sitting down for eight hours doing typing and talking to adults could be anything other than totally energising. The transition from thinking of paid work as work, to thinking of paid work as an unbelievable freaking lark is rapid for the newly minted stay-at-homer, and Shab had let himself forget that our lives had suddenly, forcibly diverged that way.

'Whacked from, you know, *work*,' he said. I stared at him, my head tilted to one side. A flicker of recognition tinged with panic moved across his face, as though he had unwittingly returned to the scene of an earlier mugging. He should know to stay away from that dark alley by now.

'I mean —' he held his palms up in surrender '— I'm not nearly as tired as you. No way. Not possible. Your days are so much more tiring than mine, totally. No contest.'

I don't know if he really meant it or whether he was trying to make a break for it after tossing his wallet and watch at my feet. His ability to truly understand my days, the minute-by-minute grind broken up by moments of Minky-related euphoria, was as limited as my ability to remember that an entire day under strip lighting in a business park can also be a little draining. He had never spent an entire week with somebody whose only social skill was pointing, and I'd never had to execute the rapid gear change that is required between leaving work at 6 p.m. and walking into the scene of utter devastation that is 6.30 p.m. in a baby-owning household. Some days, Shab would step through the front door and start narrating what he saw, like an embedded reporter in a ground war.

'It's chaos all around me here,' he'd say, holding an invisible microphone, a finger in one ear. 'It's like nothing I've seen before, just absolute carnage. I saw children's toys; they looked like they were on fire, and a woman just running. People are very, very scared.'

That night, he was too tired for it, so we settled for doing Jerry Maguire sign-language fingers in each other's faces and mouthing the words 'You deplete me.'

You've got to laugh or — the end of that phrase is 'you'll cry', I know, but it ought to be 'or you'll end up hating the one person who is legally obligated to help you'. And that would be a shame. I really didn't want to hate Shab. Hearing his keys in the door any night of the week, and especially Friday, was the unfailing highlight of my day. I still think a stay-at-home mother looks forward to the weekend more than any other person on earth and I say that knowing there are hospital cleaners working night shifts and people who sit in toll booths five days a week burning for Friday night. For a mother, though, two whole days with some help and another adult — well, that's *really* something to look forward to.

Saturday mornings felt like a miracle every single week. Chat on tap! No Click! Hours spent in a cosy three-person nest on the sofa with pillows, tea and newspapers, then a walk through Hyde Park with Minky in the Björn strapped to him and not me, so that he and not I had to contend with 'fire shoulders', that particular ache that comes with hanging an eight-kilogram infant off your trapezius with two strips of canvas. I would bounce along beside him with my hands in my pockets, chatting, planning, taking pictures, narrating Minky's every tiny development, feeling just as carefree and light as a button. We would get coffee, go out for lunch, buy books and meet the child-free friends who were dead to me for the rest of the week. Walking home through the park, couples would catch sight of our little trio, smile broadly at Shab, then at Minky, then back at each other in way that was going to get them *well* pregnant.

It was heaven — but only, it has to be said, after we honed our weekend routine and defused the marital land mines that a new baby plants in the domestic realm. A lot of new parents, for example, take turns giving each other sleep-ins on the weekend. One partner gets up early on Saturday with the baby while the other has an extra hour in bed, and vice versa on Sunday. We tried it, and it put us right inside the relational hurt locker.

Shab would take the first shift, watching every minute pass from 5.50 a.m. until 8.17 a.m., thinking '*Boy*, she is going to be grateful when she wakes up.' Points were added to one side of the parenting ledger while I dozed unknowingly. When I finally woke up, I was deeply in debt. Shab would dance from one foot to another beside the bed, awaiting praise. 'How was it? Do you feel amazing? I'm exhausted but I'm so glad you got some sleep. Seriously, do you feel *amazing*?' I did not. When a person is deeply sleep deprived, a couple of extra hours in bed are like a tiny drink of wine for a recovering alcoholic. I wanted more, desperately. I wanted to sleep all weekend. The too-short sleep-in made me feel cotton-mouthed and woozy, even more aware of what I was missing, instead of all caught up and fresh. Sunday morning, it was my turn, and if Shab's sleep-in was significantly shorter or longer than mine, we carried a mightily unbalanced ledger into a new week. Better, fairer, to just get up together and feel equally rubbish until we'd each had a turn drinking directly from the Nespresso machine like it was a school bubbler.

The sleep-ins ended anyway once we decided to go to church on Sunday mornings. I don't understand why everyone, including Satan worshippers and atheists, does not go to church once they have babies. There is *free childcare there*. You can kip through the entire service while your baby is cared for in a perfectly appointed crèche, full of toys that are sterilised each week by a lovely rostered lady. Then somebody will bring you a slice of cake on a paper serviette and point you towards a servery window where, word is, there's tea or coffee. Tea *or* coffee, did you hear what I just said? You won't believe me until you see the open canister of Moccona and a Twinings sampler box with your own disbelieving eyes, but I promise, the rumour is true. If you had extended family living near you, I suppose you would go there on the weekends instead, and doting grandparents would bring you cake and mind your child. Since we didn't, we made church its proxy, and I suggest that if you're also a mother without nearby family, try it, even if you feed earphones up your sleeve and listen to a Richard Dawkins podcast during the sermon. It is also endlessly amusing to see how a little exposure to organised religion early on impacts children's understanding of their world.

'Mum,' Minky asked me after her first term in proper Sunday School, 'what's the fastest thing in the whole entire world?'

'Oh, um, I suppose the speed of light maybe?' I said. 'Which is when light travels —'

'Yeah,' she cut me off. 'I think it's Jesus, running.'

Church was also fertile ground for, if not friend making, then at least marriage-of-convenience-style date fixing. I had already promised myself after the failed Do Nothing experiment that I would never go to bed on a Sunday night without at least three firm fixtures, real or invented, in my diary for the following week, and church was jammed with other mothers. During the period of chatting after the service, I would skate around the building with my Moleskine out, like an aggressive UNICEF campaigner on the High Street, trying to lock in dates for the week ahead. Although it cost me a small amount in the self-respect department, it bought me much more in the not-wanting-to-kill-myself-on-Monday-morning department. I never met a keeper but I killed a whole lot of separate hours. Once, I met a South African woman who had just moved to London with her three children and was on the verge of a complete unspooling. Incipient mental breakdown made her great company; she made me feel super-sane and she was always free. In South Africa, she'd had help, *help*-help, the kind that irons your bath towels for 1 rand an hour while you play tennis. Even though the oldest of her three children was six, she had never looked after them by herself before or done laundry or made dinner, let alone all at once, and she was getting hammered.

'How ah you coping with all the werk?' she asked. 'You know, all the dishes and the bins and the ah-ning. Oh ma gorsh, the ah-ning. It's indliss, is it?'

For her, dishes and ah-ning seemed like new and horrible inventions that no married couple had ever had to grapple with before. Actually, she was just experiencing late the same shock most couples encounter right after birth, when household chores instantly, exponentially increase. There is suddenly too much to do and still only two of you to do it. When Minky was four, she came into the kitchen to ask if I'd play with her. I was stirring Bolognese and defrosting the freezer while on hold with the RTA.

'I'd love to' — not true — 'but I've got to change the beds when I've finished this.'

'Aw Mum, you've always got *so much jobs*,' she said, flopping back to her room.

There *are* always so much jobs, and however the labour was divided before, the entire domestic arrangement requires a point-by-point re-examination once 'Baby Makes Three!', as the advertisement for a new-parents course, tacked up on the community noticeboard outside church, branded that period. I signed us up, after one too many arguments that began with 'Could you possibly load the dishwasher?' and ended 20 minutes later with 'We should never have got married.'

Baby Makes Three! was held in a room above a pub on the river, in Hammersmith, and run by an excessively healthy-looking couple in their late forties. She was a social worker, he a nurse, and both had bleached-out blonde buzz cuts and deeply tanned skin that suggested weekends spent doing mutually enjoyable outdoorsy things. They had raised four daughters — 'all still speaking to us!' — and had a wealth of first-hand information to impart about the spousal hazmat zone that is domestic life post-bebes. There was a makeshift podium and a miniature microphone set up in front of a semicircle of chairs. Off to one side was a folding table with a cask of white wine, a tube of plastic cups and a platter of cheese and crackers, which were noticeably too small for the giant chunks of cheddar that had been cut with only a butter knife and excessive will. Shab and I loaded up napkins with a kilo each of wensleydale and a small biscuit, and sat down with a Baby Makes Three! workbook, which we would fill in over six Wednesday nights. Minky slept in her capsule on the floor beside us while we listened to the introduction and tried to close our mouths around the outsize cheese squares without dribbling onto the exercises.

List three tasks, said Exercise One, that you don't mind doing around the house.

One. I clicked my biro on and off. 'Cooking.' Actually, I don't like cooking so much, but to let Shab make dinner is to wait until 10 p.m. and commit to talking exclusively about the dinner we are eating while we are eating it.

'I've been heavy-handed with the cumin, I think,' he'll say as I drag my starving carcass to the table.

'It's fine, honestly, it's lovely,' I assure him, my shaking hands barely able to grasp a utensil.

'Yeah, I'm not sure. Oh well. How's your rice? Mine's slightly under.'

'It's lovely, really, thanks so much for making it.'

So I kept 'cooking' and added 'grocery shopping' because it was an outing, and 'administration' because it was important sounding and general enough that if held to account later when the electricity got switched off and our passports expired, I could deny that those particular tasks were ever part of the remit.

I glanced over at Shab's side of the book, where he had written 'helping' and 'general stuff' with obvious haste so he could skip straight to the way-funner next question.

List three things you'd like to change about your partner's approach to household tasks. 'I would love it if she never again asked me what I am doing when I disappear for five minutes. Chances are, I have not opened a beer and turned on the TV. Chances are, I am doing jobs.'

He kind of had a point. I *had* developed a tendency to check up on him at all times in case he was shirking. I had coupled it with a — you say annoying, I say informative — habit of narrating my every move so he knew I was always doing jobs.

'I'm just sorting out the plastics drawer,' I would call out from the kitchen after losing visual contact with him for ten minutes.

'Don't worry,' he would call back, his head deep inside the tumble dryer. 'I don't for a second assume you're not working really, really hard all the time.'

I leaned in to whisper that we never should have got married, when the male instructor stopped circulating amongst couples and returned to the front of the room.

'Oh, whoops! Is this on? Great, OK. Pens down! Well, I hope, when you compared answers, there were some commonalities there, to give you an idea of where you can help each other out,' he said, giving a broad double thumbs-up to the floor.

'It's so important to communicate over these things because otherwise, otherwise it can eat away at your togetherness, at your ...' He searched for the right word. It didn't come. 'At your ... we-ness.'

That was it! Shab and I had been letting domestic chores eat away at our we-ness! It was surprising we had any we-ness left after so many months of unrelenting we-ness eating. It was time to stop resisting, tallying and bartering, and just get on with it. There would always be too much jobs. One of us would always feel like we were doing more than our share, simply because there was too much for two people. It's just the nature of things after Baby Makes Three!

'I promise I won't demand a brass band next time I cook,' Shab said as we walked home along the river, Minky still snoozing helpfully while her parents smoothed out their knots.

'I promise not to ask what you're doing when I can't see you,' I said, earnestly. 'I will just assume you are always doing jobs.'

'Nothing should be allowed to interfere with my we-ness,' Shab said, squeezing my hand.

'Our we-ness, Shab, *our* we-ness.'

We would need every shred of we-ness we could muster in the coming months, when Shab was made redundant. That was a fun detour off the main road of Keeping It Together, but I'm saving up all fiscal goodness, including redundancies, parking tickets, walking around money and No Fruit Mondays, for a chapter that I am planning to call 'Insufficient Funds' or possibly 'Transaction Declined'. It was the final sign, as though we needed one, that London wasn't perhaps the best place for us to raise a baby. After some touch-up paint and half a day's hire of a wet vac, we managed to sell the perch. Finally, thankfully, it was time to bubble wrap the white noise machine and the only pooper-scooper ever purchased by a non–dog owner and go home. I said goodbye to Lizzie and Emily, because, despite all those wrong-footed attempts on my part, they had provided the tiny bit of company I had had in London, and I would miss them very much. I took a last, long walk around Kensington Gardens with Minky and secretly whispered 'Thank you' to every tree that I had watched form buds after that first leafless winter, blossom and then turn into a dense canopy of green that we had spent so many hours sitting under, intentionally coping. We were leaving on an early-morning flight, and booked a taxi to take us to the airport. One of the many attractive features that the estate agent had underlined on the advertisement for Flat 4, 39 Charleville Road, West Kensington, was its easy access to Heathrow Airport via the A4. You just go up North End Road, turn left when you get to a row of bollards, and never look back.

8

OTHER MOTHERS

FOR THE FIRST YEAR OF MINKY'S LIFE, I AVOIDED ORGANISED groups of other mothers as much as possible. Here is why:

To: Bradford, Jenny [jenandscott1@hotmail.com]; Whitwell, Marie [mazza_77@gmail.com]; Sutcliffe, Jo [sutcliffej@det. nsw.edu.au]; Wong, Karen [karen_j_wong@gmail.com]; Hunter, Louise [thehunterfamily@bigpond.com.au]

From: Preston, Lisa [hollysmumlisa@yahoo.com.au]

Date: Friday, 8 January 2010, 7.42 p.m

Subject: Ladies night next wek??!!

Hey Ladies!!!!!!

Some of us were saying at group last week that it's time for a girls night out!! :-). We thought about going to that new Thai place on Fraser Street and then, for those of us who want to kick on, ;-o, to Bar Contessa for drinks afterwards!!!!! We were thinking either this Thursday (14th), next Tuesday (19th) or the following Friday (22nd) although that's the Friday before a long weekend so some of us might be going away? Anyway, if you're coming, please let me know by Monday so I can make a reservation.

Luv,

Lisa. Xxxo

PS. Can someone forward this to Mel? I only have her old address.

From: Preston, Lisa [hollysmumlisa@yahoo.com.au]

Date: Friday, 8 January 2010, 7.44 p.m.

Subject: Fwd: Ladies night next wek??!!

Obviously I meant 'week'

X Lise

That's part of it. But there's more:

Reply All: Preston, Lisa [hollysmumlisa@yahoo.com.au]; Bradford, Jenny [jenandscott1@hotmail.com]; Sutcliffe, Jo [sutcliffej@det.nsw.edu.au]; Wong, Karen [karen_j_wong@gmail.com]; Hunter, Louise [thehunterfamily@bigpond.com.au]

Cc: Nichols, Mel [info@bouncingbubhampers.com.au]

From: Whitwell, Marie [mazza_77@gmail.com]

Date: Saturday, 9 January 2010, 6.15 a.m.

Subject: Fwd: RE: Ladies night next wek??!!

Sounds great! I can do the Thursday or Tuesday but not the Friday because Johnno has a leaving do for his Brisbane boss. Hope that works for everyone? Ps will we be getting the banquet? If so, I think the Thai place by the library has a better (cheaper!!! ;-)) option. Johnno went there for work recently and said it was really good.

Cheers,

Maz

And this:

Reply All: Preston, Lisa [hollysmumlisa@yahoo.com.au]; Bradford, Jenny [jenandscott1@hotmail.com]; Whitwell, Marie [mazza_77@gmail.com]; Sutcliffe, Jo [sutcliffej@det. nsw.edu.au]; Wong, Karen [karen_j_wong@gmail.com];

Cc: Nichols, Mel [info@bouncingbubhampers.com.au]

From: Hunter, Louise [thehunterfamily@bigpond.com.au]

Date: Saturday, 9 January 2010, 4.13 p.m.

Subject: re: Fwd: RE: Ladies night next wek??!!

hi everyone. its definately [*sic*] time for the boy's [*sic*] to babysit the bubbas for a nite LOL. count me in. i can

do any night. ive [*sic*] herd [*sic*] mixed things about Thai
Fusion tho' , i know a friend who got really sick from the
masaman [*sic*] there??

Lou xoxo

And this:

Reply All: Preston, Lisa [hollysmumlisa@yahoo.com.
au]; Bradford, Jenny [jenandscott1@hotmail.com];
Whitwell, Marie [mazza_77@gmail.com]; Wong, Karen
Wong [karen_j_wong@gmail.com]; Hunter, Louise
[thehunterfamily@bigpond.com.au]
Cc: Nichols, Mel [info@bouncingbubhampers.com.au]
From: Sutcliffe, Jo [sutcliffej@det.nsw.edu.au]
Date: Sunday, 10 January 2010, 7.32 p.m.
Subject: re: re: Fwd: RE: Ladies night next wek??!!
That sounds great Lisa but unfortunately I won't be able
to make it. Riley still has a dream feed at 10pm. Thanks
anyway. See you next week.

Regards, Jo

And this:

Reply All: Preston, Lisa [hollysmumlisa@yahoo.com.au];
Whitwell, Marie [mazza_77@gmail.com]; Sutcliffe, Jo

[sutcliffej@det.nsw.edu.au]; Karen [karen_j_wong@gmail.com]; Hunter, Louise [thehunterfamily@bigpond.com.au],

Nichols, Mel [info@bouncingbubhampers.com.au]

Cc: Nichols, Mel [info@bouncingbubhampers.com.au]

From: Bradford, Jenny [jenandscott1@hotmail.com]

Date: Sunday, 10 January 2010, 7.42 p.m.

Subject: RE: re: re: Fwd: RE: Ladies night next wek??!!

Hi girls,

Sorry for the slow reply. Have been a crazy week - Piper has both bottom teeth coming through and I think she caught Holly's cough last week Lisa!!! Ugh!. Would love to do girls night. Can only do the Friday though. I'm easy re Thai Fusion or the other one, as long as they both do veggie? Also Jo, shouldn't Riley have dropped the dream feed by now? I think Gina Ford said to phase it out by 9mths?

Lots of love Jen

And, most of all, this:

To: Bradford, Jenny [jenandscott1@hotmail.com]; Whitwell, Marie [mazza_77@gmail.com]; Sutcliffe, Jo [sutcliffej@det.nsw.edu.au]; Wong, Karen [karen_j_wong@gmail.com]; Hunter, Louise [thehunterfamily@bigpond.com.au]; Nichols, Mel [info@bouncingbubhampers.com.au]

From: Preston, Lisa [hollysmumlisa@yahoo.com.au]

Date: Monday, 11 January 2010, 7.04 a.m.

Subject: <no subject>

Hi again girls. it looks like the dates don't line up so we might leave it at this stage and try again after the long weekend. Holly is still having a dream feed as well but I just keep her wrapped and she resettles really quickly. I think it should be child-led and not set in stone by some so-called expert who doesn't even have children. ;-{ See everyone Thursday. If it's raining we'll do downstairs at Pregos, but otherwise, see you on the grass outside the council. Xx

P.s. couldn't resist attaching this pic of Holly wearing Gareth's sunglasses. One for the 21st! sorry if the file size is a bit big, I don't know how to make it smaller. xxx

Omgness, stop the bleeding. There's hardly enough bandwidth in the world to cope with the surfeit of reply-all missives mothers send each other during 7 p.m. wine o'clock, as I believe, winking emoticon, it is known over at Mumsnet.

It wasn't — it isn't — that I dislike other women. I desperately *needed* the women, and a whole network of them too, not just Lizzie and one or two randoms, like I'd had in London. But I got off to a bad start with groups of mothers before Minky was even born. So bad, actually, that I'd vowed to avoid all-female assemblies in late pregnancy, and, having stuck to that hasty promise-to-self well into the first year of motherhood, I'd missed important developmental milestones where lady-friend making was concerned.

The day after I finished up at *The Times*, Emily invited me to the East Shene Leisure Centre for a swim with her, some of her friends and their toddlers. It was still unbearably hot, the tail end of the A4 summer, and although I've never done public pools, or any place, actually, where I am likely to see other people's pubic hair, either attached to or separated from their bodies, I thought it would be a good idea to reconnoitre the world of mothers and babies.

It started to go wrong before we arrived. Emily's daughter, Maeve, was one and didn't want to be in the car on such a hot day. She screamed and writhed like a trapped animal while Emily took a series of wrong turns and double-backs looking for the pool. She turned on a CD of synthesised baby songs and wound down the windows, since her little Renault didn't have air conditioning and the sun was burning into Maeve's side of the car whenever we were driving in the right direction. I sat in the front seat and tried to amuse Maeve, but twisting around to reach her with my giant stomach and facing backwards while Emily executed a bunch of hasty U-turns resulted in an unpleasant Braxton Hicks–nausea combo. When we finally arrived, the outdoor pool was crowded with teenagers, funny men sitting alone in the shallow end and what seemed like hundreds of loud, fleshy mothers and their children. On a blanket beside the kiosk, which smelled of hot chips and old people, were Emily's besties and an indeterminate number of one-year-olds.

To a mother who is yet to deliver a tiny, inoffensive newborn, there is nothing more horrific than a teething, crapping, whining one-year-old wheeling around like a drunkard with a sodden rusk in each spitty fist. The idea that the beautiful, faultless being still folded up in your uterus might turn into one of these hot-headed beasts is a grim reality check for a woman still writing letters to her unborn child in a fabric-covered journal every night. I watched in quiet horror as the mothers pulled their breasts out from inside sensible one-piece swimming costumes to placate the grizzling mega-babies, then shovelled cold mince and potato into their goopy mouths. The woman beside me exposed an areola so large and dark it looked as though she'd leaned forward into a bucket of melted chocolate. The children crawled over and through the sandwiches spread out on the rug, sucking on each other's food or grabbing handfuls of each other's faces, while others had their foul-smelling nappies changed on the same blanket. The mothers kept chatting, seemingly unconcerned about germs, or filth, or manners, or shielding their nipples from the public gaze. They loaded me up with 'just wait' topics and pieces of unwanted, too-late-anyway advice about third trimesters and feeding and the thousand terrible things that can happen to a person's vagina. All up, the outing lacked a hoped-for funness.

It was still three weeks until I would officially join their ranks and I spent every last minute of them at the Portrait Gallery, the Wallace Collection of Supremely Breakable Stuff, my own bed, any place I was sure I wouldn't come across a lactating female. It was then that I made the decision to avoid massed womanhood wherever possible. I would not join a mothers group; I would not attend a birth class; I would not let the simple fact of having a baby drag me into a cesspit of mucky white-bread sandwiches and wet-floored changing rooms in manky leisure cennahs. I would do this alone, and then some. For a year or so I did, but when one day I took a second look at a bedside table lying on the side of the road and wondered what it would look like re-varnished, I knew it was time.

Only I didn't know how, so late, to break into the world that exists inside their tightly drawn circle of strollers or, once there, fit in. To begin with, there was a language problem. A turbid gulf of lexicon stood between me and the mothers, roiling with words I just couldn't use — 'din dins', 'muzzy', 'tarnies', 'narnas' — that seemed to make up a large part of their vernacular. Even the most commonplace declension — 'bubba', 'bubs' and 'bubby' — I couldn't crack out with any conviction. Nor could I master the special conspiratorial way they had already learned to refer to their own child as 'this one', as in 'This one *loves* his veggies, don't you Cooper?' or 'This one is *so* ready to sit up.'

Some of their best-loved phrases seemed impossibly base to me. I'm not above a ripe nugget of toilet humour in normal circumstances, but hooking a finger over the elasticised waistband of your child's nappy, peering down the back and announcing that 'Harrison's filled his pants' is just so *lowering*. These women used to be lawyers! And dental hygienists and concert pianists, which made their overnight adoption of bubby talk disconcerting. 'Bubba wanna breadstick?' one would say, waving a whole-wheat grissini in front of her child's stupefied face. 'This one looooves breadsticks,' they'd explain needlessly to the nearest adult, 'don-you lil bubsa? Or is Mitchell tired? He's dropping to one sleep so he's foul by this time of day. Mitchy Moo need to go nigh-nighs, mmm? Babes, can you reach his muzzy?'

I wanted to join in. Really, by then, I was desperate. I just didn't speak the language. The year I turned 15, all I wanted in the world was to become an exchange student. I was obsessed with it the way other girls fixate on being famous or so skinny their arms get downy. A year abroad was partly about escaping tight-hat town and partly about doing something adventurous that would necessitate emotional farewell parties at both ends. I filled out all the application forms, collected character references and was accepted for a year in somewhere like Denmark, I don't remember. My parents paid the deposit and at the precise moment their cheque cleared, I realised that — *shivers!* — I couldn't speak any Denmarkian or whatever language they speak there. Talking is everything to me. It has been ever since I could talk, and I would never make it as a non-native speaker. Even if I picked up working Denmarkenese in a surprisingly short period like the exchange-student people said, I would never master sarcastic, jokey, slangy Denmarkish and be able to pepper it with references to popular culture. So I pulled out because I couldn't live without talking, and now here I was, ten years later, a non-native speaker in a foreign land I would be living in for the next decade at least. Ah, how you say ... toily?

'Don't you just talk about babies?' Shab asked one evening while we talked through my failure to assimilate.

'Yes, but it's *how* you talk about them,' I replied. 'I think I'm doing it wrong.'

Although having babies exactly the same age ought to be the ultimate conversation starter, more often it's an impediment to free and fluent chat, for the simple reason that mothers don't want to hear stories about your baby. They want to tell stories about theirs. There is a thing, apparently, when actors read through a script for the first time. They're looking for their lines, highlighter in hand, working out what's theirs, what belongs to someone else. 'Bullshit, bullshit, bullshit,' they say, scanning down the text, through pages and pages of someone else's, for a bit of theirs, 'bullshit … bullshit … MY LINE! … Bullshit, bullshit.' It's how mothers feel about anything to do with other people's children, funny things they say, the attainments and milestones thereof. Doesn't matter how funny, advanced or sweet it is, it's not my line. Whatever is going on with my face or coming out of my mouth as I listen, mentally I'm skimming the whole conversation, waiting for the bit about my baby.

'Jack had his first haircut last week,' a friend will say. Bullshit, bullshit, bullshit. 'He looks like such a little man now' — bullshit — 'but it was sad to lose all those baby curls' — bullshit, bullshit … MY LINE!

'Minky's growing hers. She calls it her "boofullonghair". She wouldn't let me touch it even if I wanted to,' I'll pitch in, while the other mother smiles, quietly thinking, 'Bullshit …'

The wonder of it all, the overarching sense of uniqueness — it's so maddening when it pertains to a child I didn't personally make. Jonathan Franzen says that nothing disturbs a feeling of specialness like the presence of other human beings feeling identically special. And mothers group is nothing if not an organised meeting of special-feeling women doing precisely the same thing. Every time I would hear a woman start in on something amazing her baby did, it made me feel less sure that Minky was as special as I'd led myself to believe. I might even start to wonder if I did, in fact, invent having babies at all. So

I would sit quietly, half-listening, thinking, 'At least I'll always have moving to London.'

Beyond the dearth of mutually satisfying talking points, the vocabulary and its witless delivery lay an even knottier discourse problem, which I eventually learned to summarise thus: these women lie. They are liars. Brazen, barefaced ones, who let a torrent of artifice spill out of their mouths in an effort to staunch the flow of self-esteem pouring from their bodies at the same rate. The lying in its hundred different forms — false compliments, exaggeration, pointed inquiry — is more understandable than all the noochy talk. You can see why it happens. In the absence of a boss, a salary or a husband who is privy to the backbreaking drudgery of it all, there is no way for an at-home mother to bolster her sense of self except through the ballsy inflation of her baby's merits. To walk into mothers group and declare outright, 'My baby is the best! My baby is better than yours!' is frowned upon, and only occasionally will a mother get close to making that kind of overt declaration. Most mothers know to couch their development talk in a kind of mock displeasure. 'Ugh, Lachie is *so* mobile, I just wish he'd slow down! I haven't even thought about baby-proofing our place,' a mother would say. Before I learned that a statement like that is a device designed to call attention to Lachie's staggering mobility, I would stare in doe-eyed confusion. Why would you want your child not to crawl? Now I would smile and ask why, if that's true, are you doing three sessions a week of Little Movers instead of tying Ziploc bags full of sand to his ankles and putting him in front of 'Waybuloo'?

Another mother will feign to share the disbelief she has wrongly attributed to you regarding her child's uncommon brilliance. And yet, while parsing the baby's talents for your benefit, she will work hard to remove any suggestion of chance. 'But then I crawled at five months, apparently,' she will say, meaning: this is not a fluke. Giftedness is deep on the ground in this family. If, for some reason, a mother hasn't bought her own line and is faltering under the weight of her baby's apparent averageness, its steady refusal to get up off the freaking 50th percentile, there is another approach available to her, as thickly iced with guile as the others. Instead of trying to dress up the scant achievements of her own little moron, she can, with the utmost politeness, cross-examine mothers with more-advanced babies in an effort to expose unfair advantage. 'Gosh she rolls well, doesn't she? How many weeks is she?' one of them will ask you. This is not a compliment. Whatever you do, don't say, 'Thank you! It's amazing isn't it?' She is not being nice. She is implying that your child has a secret rolling coach who metes out performance-enhancing S-26 Gold and trains her in salt water.

If an age difference can't explain the developmental gap, the other mother can always play the gender card ('Boys always roll late, apparently, but they're much more affectionate'), and failing that, her final recourse is to declare that the milestone in question isn't a milestone after all. 'Looks like this one is going to skip crawling all together! He just loves to stand. He always has; I think it's because his head control has always been so amazing,' she'll say, adding at the last minute, 'it's a *nightmare!*' in case she skittered too close to out-and-out boasting.

Depending on the particular blend of personalities in the group, there may also be one or two mothers of super-advanced babies who insist on dragging their trophy through the pride instead of retreating to gnaw on it in private. Their favourite contrivance is pretending that extreme giftedness is really no biggy. It doesn't mean anything, they'll falsely assure the mothers of average babies, a sentiment that were we all children in the school yard would be captured with a more succinct 'See ya, see ya, wouldn't wanna be ya.'

'It will all even out in the end, won't it?' the mother of an advanced baby will say. The failing mother, while silently worrying that it won't, lunges at the bait. 'I know, I know, it's not like when they're at school we'll be wondering who rolled at three months and who didn't!' she says. If wishing made it so. In five years, the same mothers will be sneaking sideways looks at other children's home readers to see what level they're on. This doesn't end. And always, always, there will be one mother who purports to be loving the entire business of motherhood Just *loving* it. Loving it *stupid*. Only, she won't out herself until you've just rounded out an eight-minute monologue on how motherhood has made you so miserable you've lately come to regret your child's conception. Silent until that moment, she will look at you sympathetically and say: 'I wouldn't change it for the *world*.' She may even press her own pre-verbal infant into corroborating her story. '*We* wouldn't change a thing,' she will say into her stroller, 'would we, Josie?' Sisters, she is lying. She would so change it! She might not *swap* it, but unless she is some kind of super-womby masochist, she would surely make it easier and less tiring, less fattening and less boring. She would build in more instant and visible rewards for all the daily toil, instead of balancing the entire thing on the remote and intangible fact that, if she tries hard, her child may leave her care with no criminal record or fillings. If she says otherwise, she is *lying*, isn't she, Josie?

It's an exhausting point-counterpoint, which the coffee and thick slice of apple and walnut log do not go far enough to mitigate. The baby talk, the developmental jousting, everything being an effing competition are sure things; I've never attended a gathering of three or more mothers where these talking points were not raked over endlessly and to the exclusion of all other topics. Occasionally a novice will try to get something going on the situation in the Middle East but will, for her trouble, receive dirtier looks than if she turned up to group wearing bike shorts and an undone nursing bra.

So for a long time, the foreignness of it all kept me away. I got by with Lizzie and Emily and the bits of chat I could score in playgrounds and church. Pick-up chat was easier to find once Minky became of swing-and-slide age; every day, I would hit the park and hope there'd be a half-decent broad there, someone I could talk to for 45 minutes about the NHS safety net or celebrity baby names. It definitely filled a gap, although pick-up chat is not without its own hazards. Because I'd have no background on the stranger I was over-sharing with, topics had to stay light and neutral, lest we stumble into an awkward clash of ideals: their child was eating ham straight out of the blister pack; I'd read a lot lately about how sodium nitrate causes cancer. Differences of that kind cannot be talked around easily and, in the end, one of us would need to think up a reason to go stand somewhere else without seeming rude. Plus, if it had been too long between drinks, chat wise, there was a strong chance that all my pent-up material would come pouring out at once and knock a woman who was just looking to shoot the shit right off her feet. To try and get a serious rap session going with a non-consensual mother always left me feeling a little emptied out and skanky, and ultimately a hook-up is no substitute for a real relationship. Once we were back in Sydney — with no Lizzie, no Emily and a Snooch who selfishly insisted on having a day job — I knew that I had to find the real deal. No more meaningless one-day stands. I needed serious mother-friends in large numbers, and finding them would require total dedication and an absolute surrendering of reserve.

Because Minky was already one by the time we got back, I couldn't join a proper mothers group, the kind set up by early childhood clinics. The doors close on those coven-like societies within weeks of birth and I had missed my moment. There was playgroup, but like internet dating, I held that as a last resort. Before then, I decided to sign up to classes: baby gym, music, anything that wasn't food- or nutrition-related, because, I don't know if you know this, but I was already kind of a big deal in that department. I figured that at a class I would get to see the same women over and over; we could build some rapport and, depending on how it went, take things to the next level.

Minky and I signed up for baby swimming lessons, and when my mother flew to Sydney to visit, she came along to watch. My mother was across the search for compadres and was pretty sure that this Mums 'n' Bubs water class was going to provide the solution. It was not unlike the holidays we would take to various resorts when I was a doughy preteen with breast buds that didn't yet warrant a bra and my mother would push me from behind towards a group of actual teenagers and insist I 'play with them'. When we arrived at the pool, my mother began pointing to different women and saying, audibly I felt, 'What about her?' I kept my head bowed, pretending to look for something under the stroller, which was the adult equivalent of tween-me turning up my waterproof Walkman and rolling my eyes. To make her stop, I carried Minky to the water and smiled engagingly at one of the younger-looking mothers. I had already learned, in London and again in Sydney, to steer clear of the really sag-faced women with grey hair, varicose veins and IVF twins, because they would assume I was the nanny and outright pretend not to hear me when I spoke. This woman looked nice. She was holding a little boy about the same age as Minky on her lap in the children's area. I waded over to where she sat, and looked back to my mother, who was sitting on the bleachers, nodding her head towards the woman so vigorously it seemed her neck might be broken.

'Hi there,' I said to the young mother talking contently to her son.

'Hello,' she said, looking at me. She had a strong accent, something maybe Scandinavian.

'How old is your little one?' I asked.

'He is 13 munss,' she said politely, before turning back to her boy.

'Oh right, this one is 14 months,' I said self-consciously, trying out the still-new vocabulary. 'Are you here for the Tadpole class?'

'We are here from Sweden on holiday. We are going home tomorrow.'

She knew what I was trying to do and she wasn't having it.

'Well, enjoy your trip. Bye buddy,' I said, as though her son and I had somehow managed to establish a more meaningful connection in those same 18 seconds and were genuinely sorry to part ways. I swished Minky over to the other side of the pool. My mother was nodding towards another unsuspecting victim but I felt overcome by the realisation that not every woman goes to the pool to meet people. Some are just there for the swimming.

It was time for playgroup, that shameless maternal meat market that draws every kind of desperate hausfrau and her offspring. I found one in our neighbourhood and paid for ten visits upfront so that I couldn't back out if it blew. Which it did. We were renters now, and in Sydney renting is regarded as an embarrassing personal failing on par with, say, poor depilation in New York. I had unwittingly chosen a playgroup populated entirely by amateur property developers. Every woman there except me was in the midst of a large-scale renovation, and when infant development topics had been exhausted, conversation moved to plaster dust and tiles. Which tiles? Which colour for the grout? Which tiler? My only interaction with tiles now was scraping dried food off rented ones and I had little to contribute. No-one thought it was rude to begin a conversation by asking if 'you own or ... ?' the alternative so unspeakable it was always left hanging.

'What is wrong with us?' I called to ask Shab straight after playgroup. Every week. 'Why aren't we renovating? WHY DON'T WE HAVE A D.A. IN?'

'Hang on,' he'd say. 'Just checking. Yes, here we are. Thursday, twelve-fifteen. This conversation is right here in my diary.'

I decided to run out my ten paid-up visits, while throwing the net wider — other playgroups, library toddler mornings, church groups — and eventually, invitations to play dates and park trips began to trickle in. I said yes to all of them. In the course of a few months, I teamed up with every kind of baby-lady. Rich mothers whose white linen sofas I was too scared to sit on, mothers so flaky and out of whack with their children's routines I didn't know if they'd turn up at 7 a.m. or 4.50 p.m. Women wound tighter than Martha Stewart in her last week in prison; others who didn't seem to notice or care that their dog was licking the baby's mouth. Sometimes I went back for second visits, and once or twice I even agreed to try out the 5 p.m. Friday barbecue with the husbands, only to discover that the glimmer of attraction we'd experienced at 9 a.m. on a wet library day didn't translate to the men, who weren't nearly as crazed for chat, and that's just a waste of the second-cheapest kind of Jacob's Creek. I struck up a thing once with a woman from a bookshop story hour. She invited Minky and I over for a play one Monday morning and we went. 'Now,' she explained as we walked from the front door to the family room, 'I'm going to the airport in five — I've got a work trip — but Dad's here looking after the kids, so you're welcome to stay and watch a

DVD with him.' Not Dad as in her husband, which would have been only medium-awkward. Dad as in her own aged father, who turned and waved from the sofa, where he sat by himself watching 'Boo!' on mute.

Later I swapped details with a woman from a council playgroup, whom I had privately nicknamed Double Denifer because her day-to-day uniform was an unbecoming denim skirt and a jean jacket and her real name was Jenifer — you see what I did there. She reeled me in with a pretty funny riff on how she'd nearly killed herself having two children 13 months apart. 'Irish twins,' she called them. Because of their non-concurrent sleep times — the younger baby was still on two short sleeps, morning and afternoon, while the older baby had one long one just exactly in between — she hadn't stepped outside her own front door for 22 months and was just getting back on the circuit. Denifer wore no make-up, only a thick smear of factor 40 toddler sunscreen, which made her entire face glow with the milky translucence of a cultured pearl. A lot of times, the cream migrated into her hair, making her look greasy around the temples, but I was willing to overlook some bad personal grooming choices in the search for company. She invited me over to her house for morning tea, which is kind of second base, and maybe I should have suggested we take it slow and try a park first, but she seemed eager to host and I agreed. I texted her on the way over to see if she wanted a coffee.

'I'll B naughty + have a skim cap, no chocolate!!!!!' she texted back, four seconds later.

I found her house, parked, lifted Minky out of the car seat and carried her on my hip up Denifer's front path. Like a deserted battlefield, the lawn was strewn with the remnants of war — faded plastic scooters and a Little Tikes kitchen lying on its side, with weeds growing out of the microwave and slimy rainwater pooling in the corner of the sink. I knocked and heard some scuffling and toddler-whining from inside. Denifer threw open the door, her SPF-y face lighting up an otherwise pitch-dark vestibule. 'Don't mind the mess!' she chirruped, as we picked our way down the hall, littered with knotted nappy sacks, children's sandals, a double stroller half collapsed and a baby bag the size of a hay bale. I didn't mind the mess; I could hardly see the mess through the PND-inducing gloom of her cave-like hall.

I sat down at the kitchen table, which was covered with a sweaty plastic cloth and stacked with 22 months worth of washing, craft and unopened mail. Denifer pushed it all to one side with both arms, like an angry boss about to clean-sweep an employee's desk. She set down a dinner plate onto which she had fanned out a whole packet of Milk Arrowroot biscuits. Beside it she placed an open can of pineapple rings and two forks. I guess in Denifer's mind we were going to fork-dive into the can together, like two après-skiers eating fondue. I took our coffees out of the cardboard tray and tried to think of anything at all that I could talk about with this suddenly alien woman. In the other room a television was tuned to one of the morning shows. Her oldest child, Callum, stumbled into the kitchen wearing no nappy, just Velcro sandals and a onesie with the flaps undone. She pulled him up on her lap, and as he lay back to suck on an Arrowroot, his toe-sized pip peeked out from behind the onesie flaps in a way that was totally disconcerting to the mother of a girl.

As well as being a hater of switching on a light ever, Denifer also appeared not to be a fan of fresh air. It was a warm summer day outside, but the kitchen windows stayed shut and bolted behind the drop-down verticals that the younger child kept trying to pull himself up on just behind my chair.

'No, Liam! Ugh, this one is desperate to start cruising,' Denifer moaned, as she got up to untangle him from the beaded cord. As she passed by me on her way to the baby, she plonked Callum and Callum's naked pip onto my lap in an unwelcome gesture of sorority. I was wearing shorts and was instantly terrified that if Callum's horrifying boy luggage accidentally touched my bare thigh, it might qualify as 'bad touching'. I was too scared to adjust him while we were both seated, since he was heavy and if I raised my pelvis to tip him forward it could look worse, like a jerky little thrust. I turned my head away and tried to swallow back the strangling claustrophobia of having somebody else's sticky toddler sitting on my lap in this dark, airless kitchen. A fly, I noticed, was trying to suicide against Denifer's ranch slider.

I'd been duped. This woman was not a kindred, and I was going to pay the price for letting desperation cloud my judgement. She had reeled me in with the 'Irish Twins' bit. Now, as she talked me through the how, when and why of Liam's night-poo situation, I realised 'Irish Twins' was a set piece, a standard opener that she'd perfected and used over and over like a tour guide who loves the laughs and knows exactly where they'll come. She delivered the entire spiel again just after 'Night Poo': 'Twelve months and twenty-four days apart exactly — my midwife actually said, "See you next year" when I left hospital, and I said, "Over my dead body," HAR HAR HAR HAR.' I sipped my coffee and reached down to pat Minky, who was sitting on my foot, motionless. I think now that if I'd interrupted Denifer partway through ' … it must have happened the first time Gary and I did it after Callum came …' she would have had to start again from the beginning.

As soon as it seemed polite, or maybe a fraction before that, I started to wrap things up.

'Well, this has been lovely,' I said.

'Oh, don't go! You've only just arrived. I thought I'd make us some lunch in a bit.'

It was 10.30 a.m. I was beginning to feel like the writer in *Misery* who keeps getting his legs broken by his psychotic fan-captor. Actually, in a certain light, or the complete lack of, Denifer looked not unlike a young Kathy Bates, coated in lotion.

'You don't want us to stay!' I said imploringly. 'It looks like you've got your hands full here anyway,' I added as Denifer hoisted Liam up onto the table to put a nappy on him, in standing-up position, right there next to the can of pineapple. My stomach did a little flip. 'Anyway, I need to get home before Minky falls asleep in the car.'

'Oh, she doesn't look tired to me!' Denifer insisted. 'I thought she could have her sleep here while we chat. I've set up the Portacot in my room.' An image of her and Gary doing it leaped into my head — that denim skirt rucked up around her waist. I felt weak, and since I'd been scrabbling around for conversation starters since just after the 'Don't mind the mess' of 37 long, painful minutes before, I was more than sure I didn't have the two to four hours of additional chat that Denifer was obviously primed for. If I didn't shut this relationship down asaps, next thing we'd be late-night shopping at Just Jeans while the 'boys did the kids'.

It was starting to get out of hand, so I did something I'd only ever done once before, during a pregnancy massage when I became overwhelmingly convinced just after I lay down that the masseur was going to do bad touching. I faked a phone call.

'Oh, excuse me, Jenifer, my phone is vibrating.' It wasn't. 'Hi, darling. That's terrible. Yes, definitely, I can come right down.

I'll be there in ten minutes.' I fake-hung-up. 'Sorry, that was my husband. He's at work and has got terrible food poisoning; I said I'd go and get him. We'll have to do that lunch another time,' I added, knowing that I would cut my hair and move cities before I ever let this woman learn my whereabouts again.

'Yes!' Denifer agreed. 'I'll just get my diary. Tomorrow or the next day,' she said, flipping through the empty pages, 'or the next day is good for us — what about you?'

'Gosh, I feel like I've got something on tomorrow, I just can't remember what,' I said, scooping up Minky and feeling my way along the wall to the door. I felt bad; I didn't want to see the empty diary, the plastic tablecloth or the fly attempting to self-harm, but the damage was done. Denifer wasn't a bad person; we just weren't a match. All that was left was a lesson in character assessment and a little bit less will to live on both sides.

Denifer and I never did manage to hook up for lunch. I think her number might have fallen out of my phone, weirdly, right before I started shopping around for a different playgroup. A few years later I saw her again, at the beach. Her entire family was standing on the sand, coated in incandescent white sun cream. The husband and the boys were wearing long rashies over Speedos, which brought into my mind, like a post-traumatic flashback, Callum's open flaps and that tiny skin-coloured champignon lying against my leg. Denifer frowned and pretended not to recognise me. I did the same, even though I'd sat in this woman's kitchen and tried to catch a slippery, heavy pineapple ring on a fork and eat it out of politeness.

On my last prepaid session at Renovators Not-the-Least-Bit-Anonymous, I noticed a woman I hadn't seen before. She was sitting on a folding chair with a polycup of milky tea, listening to someone's pool-tile-installation drama with the wryest, fakest, boredest smile on her face. She had a daughter the same age as Minky. We swapped numbers and the following week arranged to meet at a playground with no renovators in it. She was a keeper. The first proper friend I made in Australia. Every Thursday morning from then on, we met in that park and took turns getting the coffee. As the weeks, then months, then years went by, we workshopped illness, redundancy, mothers-in-law, preschool, work, morning sleeps, theology, answering back, books, clothes and a thankfully mutual shortness of cash, while our children played or silently bit each other. In summer we baked in that park and in winter we froze, but she was always there and so was I, with two large lattes and a week's worth of dot points. The reason we became such firm friends, I think now, is because she has a similar personality to Shab, all the same calm, nonjudgemental Yin to balance out my flighty, sharp-tongued Yang, which also explains her nickname, Girl-Shab.

Sometimes we would get too absorbed and the children would get into maybe the tiniest spot of bother. 'So anyway, we're in Woolworths,' I was saying to Girl-Shab one day, 'and Minky leaned out of the trolley towards this plumber guy lining up in front of us.' Girl–Shab was riveted (bullshit, bullshit). It was a great story, totally unique, about how Minky had reached out and tried to insert her index finger into the top inch of exposed ass cleavage belonging to the tradesman in front of us. 'She's always been really advanced at those toys where you put the blocks into the slots, so —'

'DOES ANYONE KNOW WHOSE CHILD THIS IS?' a mother shouted over me, holding a screaming Minky under the arms, away from her own body. My daughter's face was thickly breaded with sand, tears, the banana she'd been eating before she fell face first into the sandpit and a little blood from hitting the edge on the way down. 'DOES ANYONE KNOW WHERE HER MOTHER IS?'

'Oh … um … she's mine,' I said, sheepishly. 'Sorry. Thank you. I was just telling my friend here about the time when …' Bullshit.

9

HOME, HELP,

THERE IS A PARTICULAR KIND OF RELIEF I FEEL WHEN I HAVE been in the kitchen forever frying something very smoky and feeling the whole time tense and shouty. Then, when it's done, I remember I can turn off the kitchen exhaust fan now and aah, so quiet. *That's* why I was feeling so het up, the perpetual low-grade whirring in my ear this whole time. That sort of relief, times a gajillion, is how I felt when we finally left London, in 2004. The permanent drone of crowds and yelling and pigeons and three o'clock darkness, other people's rage and my own miserable internal monologue was suddenly, as though a switch had been flicked, gone. Aah, so quiet.

The relief was heightened by the fact that just before we left London, we'd inadvertently signed up for one final round of punishment, a four-day weekend away with Lizzie and Max and three other families they knew and we didn't. Max, as it happened, has relatives who own a 15th-century castle deep in the Hertfordshire countryside. He arranged for us all — we were eight adults and eight children altogether — to stay in the refurbished outbuildings for a long weekend. I was excited because we had been out of London only once since Minky was born, for her first Christmas. I had forced all three of us onto a last-minute flight to Prague on Christmas Eve because, despite my most fervent prayers and machinations, I hadn't found anywhere for us to spend the day and the idea of passing our daughter's first Christmas alone in a West Kensington flat was a total wrist-slitter. I remember almost nothing about those two peculiar nights in the Czech Republic, except for the cab ride from Ruzyne Airport, which I spent attempting to express to the non-English-speaking driver, through the medium of mime, that he could not smoke in his own cab because he happened to be driving a VIB and her parents to their 3.5-star hotel.

I remember everything about the castle weekend, though, as hard as I have tried to forget it. I was nervous to begin with because I had met a lot of Lizzie's friends by then and they were even more intimidating than her. They were older and English and wealthy; Shab and I were younger, Australian and, at that moment, both unemployed. We drove up a day later than everybody else, and as we rounded one of the bends in the long gravel driveway that led up to the castle, lined each side with plane trees and daffodils, I saw a neat row of station wagons in elegant colours like dark green and navy parked in front of a building called the Long House, where we were all staying. We parked beside them in our borrowed hatch and went to find everybody. I was, by then, exceptionally nervous, suddenly convinced that coming was a terrible mistake. We were the only first-time parents. The other parents had whole broods, which made them proper families and us bumbling amateurs. If ever there is a time when you want to look like you're all over the business of parenting, it's on a shared family holiday rammed with toffs.

We found everybody assembled in the paved courtyard behind the Long House. Max made introductions: a Bertie, an Ed, some Nancys and one or two Annabelles, that's the kind of crew it was. I felt, as I waved weakly with one hand and stuffed the other deep into my jeans pocket, like an annoying younger sister who has been allowed to join an older sibling's trip to the movies. I desperately wanted to be in the club, but clearly I was not, which meant my second-best option was trying to blend in and not embarrass the person who brought me.

They were on their way out for a hike, Max explained, which was why the mothers and fathers were pulling on walking boots, threading children's arms through the sleeves of downy jackets and stowing all-terrain strollers with supplies enough for back-to-back K2 summittings. 'Oh, we'll join you!' I said, as all eyes turned to me, then dropped to the jeans and ballet flats I'd worn for the car ride.

'Are you sure you don't need to go and change first?' one of the Annabelles asked. Even if I'd wanted to, I'd only packed normal clothes, nothing with GORE-TEX or wicking capability.

'I'll be fine,' I promised, as we set off towards the fields around the castle. As it turned out, the terrain was about as rugged as the unmown sections of Hyde Park, but the first blow to my legitimacy had been struck.

That evening, we fed the children all together at 5 p.m. I spooned mushed lentils, spinach and goat cheese into Minky's mouth and tilted the bowl towards the other mothers so they could admire the contents, which I'd brought in a cooler pack from London. At six, everybody disappeared upstairs to put their offspring to bed. Our room was a little garret at the end of a long corridor. We would be sharing a bathroom with two other couples sleeping on the same floor. I put Minky to sleep in her travel cot. It was the same cot she slept in every night at home, so pleasantly familiar to her. The real novelty for her was to be in a proper bedroom, because at home, she had been sleeping in the bathroom ever since she outgrew her crib. A cot wouldn't fit in our room, so she had to move next door and into a travel cot pushed up against the bath. Let's not rake over how bad I felt about putting my daughter to sleep in a bathroom.

Let's just focus on that lovely castle room and the rare pleasure it was for her to have an entire night without a tap running or toilet flushing inches from her sleeping face.

When Minky was settled, I went back down to the living room and caught the tail end of what looked like some sort of grown-up treasure hunt. In fact, the other parents were all scrabbling around on their hands and knees looking for power points at which to dock baby monitors, which were soon stationed all over the living room, lights blinking, volume-sensing bars sensing.

'You're very brave leaving her up there with no monitor,' one of the fathers said to me. 'Very nonchalant.' I chose to take his observation at face value, since he was a man.

'Aren't I, though!' I said, not explaining that when you live in a one-bedroom flat, there's very little call for a baby monitor. You can hear crying from the adjacent bathroom fairly well just with your human ears, so we didn't own one.

We sat down to dinner, and one of the mothers poured herself a big glass of wine and started in on a story about how her daughter had come down with the most unbelievably virulent stomach bug just before they'd come away. It was the same little girl that I'd seen at the children's tea table lean across and stick a thick finger in Minky's mouth. I thought nothing more of it and enjoyed the wine and dinner and conversation, which was interrupted every ten minutes or so by a different parent scampering off to the living room and holding his or her monitor up to a cocked ear. At around 10 p.m., as empty plates were pushed into the middle of the table, a weak, stifled cry sounded from one of the monitors. Six adults leaped to their feet to see whose it was, and when its origin couldn't be determined, a pair of the most vigilant parents tripped upstairs to investigate. Five minutes later, the same father who'd been so taken with my breezy parenting style tapped me on the shoulder.

'Seems the crying is coming from your room,' he said.

'Oh, don't worry, she'll go back to sleep,' I assured him, tipping the last bit of wine into my mouth for maximum nonchalance.

A few minutes later, the crying seemed to be intensifying rather than abating. The volume-sensing bars on the monitor were flashing on and off like a caller board at a talkback radio station. I pushed my chair out from the table, rolled my eyes in a way that meant 'Kids, right?' and headed for the stairs.

When I opened the door to our room, an acrid cloud of *something* hit me square in the face. It was dark, and I leaned into the cot to feel around for Minky. The sensation was like plunging two hands into a trough of cold casserole. Minky had been sick. Violently so. It was the first time she'd ever been ill, and I felt an enormous wave of pity, guilt and remorse. I scooped her up and called out for Shab, who was already at my back. Minky had the most bewildered and apologetic look on her face, as though she was really so sorry for ruining our night.

'It's OK, it's OK. I'm so sorry, Minky, you poor thing,' I said as Shab balled up the cot sheets, ran her a bath and dug around in our bag for fresh nappies and pyjamas. We made our apologies to downstairs and, after bathing her and showering ourselves, went to bed.

At around midnight, I was woken by the sound of my own stomach. You've heard it in a hundred Farrelly brothers' films: the angry, volcanic murmurings that make you curl up and whisper, 'Please, please no,' to your own gastric system. I'll stop before the watery mouth, hot palms and emergency dash along the dark hallway. In fact, I'm not going to go into details at all — it's too gross. I'll bullet-point it instead:

- a stomach bug so ferocious I hit my head against the bathroom wall in the first throes of it
- first me, then Shab
- all night
- shared bathroom
- a desperate fear that I might die
- an even more desperate fear that I might not die
- poorly soundproofed walls, even in a 15th-century stone castle outbuilding, according to everyone the next day.

Minky was fine and back on form early the next morning, but Shab and I were both still finishing up. We took turns stumbling to the bathroom or downstairs for weak peppermint tea. We were too enfeebled from the night's labour to drive the three hours home first thing, so to avoid smiting the whole party with our bug, we confined ourselves to the garret for the whole day, feeling like death not even warmed up, with a bored baby sitting in between us, bouncing up and down. That night, with voided stomachs and shaking hands, we stuffed all our things into bin bags, including two borrowed sets of sheets we promised to launder and return in the post, and drove unsteadily home. One of us did a spell driving while the other lay down in the back seat with a lidless cake tin in the foot well. As we'd waved goodbye to the secretly horrified guests standing in the driveway, I felt an overarching sense of otherness. I felt foreign and embarrassed about being the only adults in a group of six others to come down with a child's tummy bug. And six years later, neither of us can get near peppermint tea.

'Tea?' a friend will say. 'I've got chamomile, peppermint …' they will continue, and we will shake our heads politely, thinking, 'I would prefer a cup of warm Pert.'

So, finally, we were back in our own hemisphere, with our own people. Shab and Minky and I fell through the door of my parents' house in New Zealand after the 57-hour flight and stayed for a month before setting up in Sydney. We decompressed. All-we-could-eat baby-sitting, dinners cooked by someone else, washing that would just turn up done, and not, as I had seen in the last gruesome weeks of London, with a small circle of fresh mouse droppings atop the neatly folded pile. Also, for the first time, I got to watch Minky crawl in a straight line. In our flat she'd only been able to do tight circles in the living room, like a rowboat with one oar. Seeing her go — well, it was like something out of *Born Free*, without the stirring score or lions. I was so happy to be home.

It seems to me that once you are a mother, the only time you can step out from under the weight of responsibility that is your now-permanent lot is by repairing to your own mother's house. Even if you can't stand her, even if she drives you to the very edge of coping with comments that are intended as neutral observations but come out as the pointiest kind of judgement. 'Your hair's getting long, darling,' she'll say just by the by, as you bristle in silent defence of yourself. What does she mean by that?! Even under a torrent of such remarks, being with your mother is the only time, post-babies, that you can really kick it into neutral. I made the most of it because once we settled in Sydney I would be back to day-to-day motherlessness. From there, she would be a flight away, which is no better in practical terms than the 24-hour journey that was between us before. For a mother to be useful, she really needs to live in your under-stairs cupboard and only come out when you say it's OK. Instead, for just two weeks a year my mother comes to stay, cleans my oven and, while wiping her forehead on her upper arm, says, 'Gosh, you've cooked a lot in here!' WHAT DOES SHE MEAN BY THAT? I … we just! … ugh … nothing.

Meaning, I know well the special envy a motherless mother feels towards peers who do have their mothers nearby. I don't believe for a minute that it can be as complicated, emotionally charged and all strings-attached as I've heard friends say. I just imagine help — limitless, free, the sort you don't even have to say thank you for and never have to reciprocate. If I had a mother in the same city I could indulge myself endlessly with things the motherless only dream of, like facials or bouts of illness. Until motherless mothers are ill enough to require surgery or dialysis, we don't get to be sick, in the sense of going to bed, eating soup from a tray and watching DVDs on the laptop. We just keep doing all the things we usually do, while pitching out the odd puke or bloody stool.

A while after we were settled in Sydney, I was slugging my trolley down the aisles of Woolworths with a new baby who was arching and straining against the straps of the child seat like she might actually eject herself, and a Minky who was walking not so much alongside the trolley as constantly into the side of it, so that her bright purple Croc got sucked into the wheel every, oh, five seconds. Each time, she would scream like it was a new and shocking experience. This we did once a week and I knew the routine down. I would get around the supermarket, hold my breath for the 20 seconds it took for 'Approved' to flicker up on the eftpos machine, load the car, buckle the children in, drive home, take the children out, carry them up two flights of stairs, secure them in some sorely questionable way (with television, say, or by just telling them not to move), then run up and down the stairs to the car, which we had to park on the other side of our busy road, until all 14 finger-splitting bags had been hauled inside. If, because of some disastrous miscalculation on my part, the children fell asleep in the car and could not be kept awake by my throwing empty sultana packets at them from the front, I would have to decide who to take up first and who to leave vulnerable to passing kidnappers while I did so. Bottom line, it was hard work. Not hard work of the indentured-labour-in-Sudanese-carpet-factory sort, but hard work of a kind that Gwyneth Paltrow will never have enough experience of to Goop about. 'Sometimes people ask me how I like to break my back for little or no reward on a weekly basis,' Gwyneth will never write, 'and to them I say, we busy working mamas haul ass to Whole Foods!' Most of the time, I could shut down the complaining song in my head by reminding myself that every mother I know does this once a week, twice if she's disorganised, three if she hasn't made friends yet. Grocery shopping is no fun for anybody. Toughen up, I'd tell myself.

In fact, not *everybody* does it like this. Ones with mothers of their own don't. I know because I saw it right in front of me as I

155

tried to tug a Croc out from under a trolley wheel. As I crouched there in the aisle, past me walked another mother, wearing a newborn in a sling. She was pushing the trolley, but instead of picking items off the shelves herself, she would point to what she wanted, and her mother, a woman in her mid-sixties who was walking in front, would scamper over to retrieve it. She only had to point! Her mother was doing all the heavy lifting, heaving the three-litre orange juice bottles and half-tonne bags of dog food over the side like she was sandbagging a flood levy. 'No, not that one, the bigger one,' the daughter would say, as a willing senior citizen scanned the shelves looking for the product in line with her daughter's outstretched finger.

I felt many things witnessing that piece of mother–daughter tag-teaming. I felt jealous, obviously. Where was my maternal equivalent of a seeing-eye dog? I was also curious about when the arrangement would time out and the daughter would have to start schlepping it around Woolworths single-handedly like the rest of us. And I also felt, in a funny way, proud that I could do all this for 50 weeks a year without a back-up beyond my husband. It helped that finally we were living in a place where my fall-back mood was good to quite good, rather than miserable to black despair. Sydney is a lovely place to have babies. You can go to the beach, and it's free and there's nobody there, which feels amazing for a long time after you've been trying to raise a baby in London, where the only place I'd found for a paddle was the heavily trafficked open drain that is the Diana, Princess of Wales Memorial Fountain. Shab had found a job quickly, and we moved into a flat in an Art Deco building by the harbour. It was not fancy, and I'm not going to tell you that it didn't have a serious roach problem, which was, a few months later, our reason for leaving. 'Mummy, tiny turtle on me' was all I needed to hear from Minky before I returned to the rental listings, but for six months it was a good enough base for daily outings. Minky and I took ferries to the Art Gallery, where I explained the paintings to her in a voice loud enough to garner complimentary looks from strangers. We sat on upturned milk crates the way people do here and had coffee and smoothies. I discovered that anything normal mothers do with their toddlers at home, like reading books or painting, I could do outside on a blanket under a tree, because of the ten-month summer. I worked out how to have whole days of fun on under $20, which is clever since although Sydney is many things, one of them is not cheap.

Minky was one year old, then one and a half. She started talking properly, which made me feel a little less like a crazy shut-in yammering all day to a crazy mute. We joined the zoo and spent whole days there, Minky on my shoulders, pointing out sparrows and sheep because she was never that blown away by the exotic stuff. Even with Girl-Shab on my books for Thursdays, I still woke up every other weekday with that free-falling sense of panic vis-à-vis how to fill the day, but the solo-options were more plentiful, easier to get to and not viciously oversubscribed as in London. And the sun was usually shining, so either way, I was ahead.

I found a little funny occasional-care centre that would take Minky off my hands for a whole morning and give me change from a 50. I spent those three hours trying to drum up freelance work, counting the minutes until I had to go and get her. I read *A Life's Work* again, and this time I noticed a different bit. 'When she is with them she is not herself; when she is without them she is not herself; and so it is as difficult to leave your children as it is to stay with them. To discover this is to feel that your life has become irretrievably mired in conflict, or caught in some mythic snare in which you will perpetually, vainly struggle.' Minky's initially gradual journey out of me and into the world gathered pace, and now that felt just as new and disconcerting as when she'd taken me over a year and a half ago.

Which is why we started thinking about going again, I suppose. Having another. Number Two. In London I had decided there would only be one child *pour nous*. Motherhood was beautiful and amazing and brilliant, of course, but at the very bottom, it was too hard to do over with another whole human. Then Shab, in his wise Shabby way, tabled the idea that although it might be harder in the short term, ultimately it would be more fun to have Minky plus one. Siblings and all. Bunks, punching, someone to go eeling with or daub soap onto the toothbrush thereof while they are not looking. Minky would soon be two, and as an avid doer of period/gestation/age gap maths, I decided it was now or never. I didn't want to wait until she was already at school so that the second baby would know for sure it was only born because its mother didn't want to go back to work. Also, once you're kicking around with a toddler all day, a fresh, clean, minuscule newborn who can't run the word 'Mum' up three octaves seems fantastically alluring. It was time. This was not a drill. 'Guys,' I would have said if I'd had anyone to tell, 'we're trying!'

Do you know what you do a lot of before your first baby is born? Daydream, plan, visualise little scenarios in which you are lying in bed on a Sunday morning, reading the papers and drinking tea while the baby gurgles beside you. You lie in the bath talking to your bump and accept invitations to destination weddings set for three months after your due date, because it's all a beautiful dream. Do you know what you do before your second baby? Nothing. You don't even do a pregnancy test until you're 16 weeks and your jeans start leaving red marks on your stomach. After the baby is born, you never, ever, ever, ever, ever (ever) wake it, no matter what you've read about three-hour cycles. You drink Diet Coke while you're breast-feeding and never expedite a milestone with intensive coaching and wishing and urging. In fact, when it's time to start the second baby on solids, you weep because that is one more job to do and you'd just got done with the highchair and cleaning under it so many times a day. And you will take back everything you ever said about how irresponsible it is to leave two children in the car while you run in to pay for petrol. There is another new world to discover, by just as much trial and error.

Not long after we started trying, guys, a metallic taste in my mouth and breasts like two rocks on fire told me we had succeeded. This time, I was too busy with Minky to puke or nap or sit and cry it out beside an arterial road, but still I worried late at night that this baby wasn't going to get a look-in. I worried that I couldn't love it, that we couldn't afford it, couldn't go back to those knife-edge early days of newborn-ness. That feeling is universal, I think. I've never heard a woman pregnant with her second child bray about how sure she is she's going to love this one the same, if not more than, the first. I decided to take that on advice, and the rest of my second pregnancy passed in a blur of park trips, house cleaning and chocolate milk, which I have never desired before or since but which, at the time, was the only thing I wanted ever, in quantities large enough to help me lay down a tidy 22 kilograms of baby weight. Three eventual kilos of baby, 19 kilos of thigh.

Two weeks before my due date, I was at the park chatting with some random pick-up mothers. I mentioned that, gosh, I was having trouble sleeping. My skin was like sandpaper and I lay awake every night scratching.

'Um, I think that's a *thing*,' one of the other mothers said. 'I think you should get that checked out.'

'Really? I just thought I've been having my showers too hot,' I said.

'No, it's definitely a thing,' another mother chimed in. 'You should tell your obstetrician.' Or, indeed, the randomly rostered junior resident I could look forward to seeing in the *public* health system.

Had I boned up on gestational trivia at any point in either of my pregnancies, I would have known it was a thing. But I had purchased, and long since abandoned, only one pregnancy book from the 14,000 titles available at the time of my first Clearblue. I chose *What to Expect When You're Expecting* by Heidi E. Murkoff, Sandee E. Hathaway and Arlene Eisenberg, who doesn't, for some reason, cite a middle initial. I had heard it was a classic. After work one day I stopped in to a Waterstones, found the parenting section, beyond Mental Health, Crime and Horror (all preferable life experiences according to the store's planner), scanned the predominantly pink and teal selection and picked out the last copy. I spent £16.99 on it and read it on the Tube. It fell open to a section called 'Thyroiditis Got You Down?' If I knew what thyroiditis was, I have no doubt it would have been getting me down bad. What got me down even more was the entire book, with its line drawn illustrations of body parts I did not recognise, its relentless fear mongering and, most of all, the dozens and dozens of fake Q&As that made up the bulk of this bulky tome. They were written in a tone so joyfully condescending and risk obsessed I could have been 16 again and back in my drivers' education class.

Q: *My hair seems to be falling out suddenly. Am I going bald?*
A: No need to stock up on hats!

Well, thank goodness! I was about to splash out on a dozen berets, but as the authors go on to explain, postpartum hair loss is quite normal. Still, they say, it's a good idea anyway to 'treat your hair with kindness', which means 'using a conditioner to reduce the need to untangle, using a wide-toothed comb if you *do* have to untangle [italics mine, and heaven *forfend*], and avoiding the application of heat'. Get that sandwich press off your head and start writing this stuff down, women! Did you get the bit about the conditioner? And the comb?

I heard Murkoff et al. have revised the entire book recently, adding sections on Botox use in pregnancy and belly piercing. I imagine they've also nixed the original cover, which features an illustration of a pregnant woman who looks around 85 years old sitting in a rocking chair with her hands folded smugly over her tabard. My edition, from the early 2000s, shows a woman about eight months along standing side on (can pregnant women stand any other way? it is fair to wonder) in a peach cable-knit jumper and white leggings, the perfect choice for anyone discharging the half-dozen kinds of fluids the book details in chapters 3, 4 and 5. She has her head thrown back in delight and a white suit jacket slung over her shoulder like she's just back from doing a set with Michael Bublé. The latest cover I'm sure will feature a woman in expensive yoga pants, the tabard of our time. However, unless they've also revised the entire tone and deleted the phrase 'really nothing to worry about' from the hundred or so paragraphs that describe the most worrying conditions we'd never have known about if it wasn't for their book, I can't recommend it. It did not help me before or after pregnancy; it just made me scared. I'm flicking through right now ... pain in perineal area ... rupture of membranes ... inadequate amniotic fluid ... darkened amniotic fluid ... Jewish–style delis ... sugar in the urine. I am so freaked out and I'm not even pregnant. The purpose of reading during pregnancy and forever after is to make you feel better, not worse. Plus I already know just from being a toilet-trained adult that it's important to 'empty your bladder regularly'. I don't need to be reminded by a trio of women who may or may not be doctors, just other toilet-trained adults.

To answer the itchy-skin question, I bypassed Murkoff and her homegirls and called the hospital once we left the park. 'Oh yes, you better come in. The doctor will see you immediately,' a nurse told me. After you have children, you always want doctors to laugh you out of their rooms after a talking-to about a little syndrome they call Munchausen by proxy. You never want your medical concerns to be taken seriously by the establishment, so when they are, it's a weensy bit scary. I went to the hospital, lugging Minky, who still couldn't walk in a straight line or past a fallen leaf without checking it thoroughly, and we saw the doctor. If you haven't had a vaginal exam with an inquisitive nearly-three-year-old in the room, you haven't lived. As it happened, I had cholestasis, some sort of liver problem that I would never get a chance to trace back to a Jewish–style deli or inadequate amniotic fluid because, bottom line, if I didn't deliver the baby asaps, it would turn as salty as a rollmop, and my skin would have flaked off in sheets before then. An induction was booked for the following day, and I went home to call my mother-in-law, who had flown in from New York to look after Minky, and to pack a hospital bag, another thing you don't do until the last minute second time around. Third time around I imagine you stuff some clean washing into a bin liner on the way out the door, and fourth time, come home wearing what you wore in, with your baby wrapped in a beach towel that was already in the car.

This time, also, I had used the 'Your Birthplan' section of my hospital notes as an ad hoc baby wipe for one of Minky's spills. The plan was drugs, early and often, and I didn't need to write that down to remember it. We checked in at 7 a.m., and once they wound up that drip and the contractions started in, an anaesthetist was called. Remember me getting all lovey last time? This time it was better. This time I got lovey *and* racist. When the anaesthetist arrived, I was sucking back deep lungfuls of gas and drunkenly telling Shab, whose shoulders I had slung one heavy arm around, just how much nitrous oxide tastes like Milo.

'It's soooo chocolately and milky, baby! Yoouuuu ssshould try some, this stuff is the BOMB ha ha ha ha ha oooooh hello Mr Doctor. Are you Chinese?' I asked with mock seriousness as the door swung open.

He was.

'Ooh Shab ssshhh,' I hushed him with a slappy hand to his lips, even though he was not actually speaking, forcing his head backwards with my ill-judged force. 'Listen, shh, the doctor is sssshinese. That isss very good and do you know why, baby? They are hard *workers*.' I thought I was whispering. Whispering like a drunk teenager trying to get a key in the front door at 3 a.m. without waking her parents maybe.

'They are such hard workers. In their culture, Shab,' I continued. 'So he is going to be so good at doctoring. I wonder if he — sssh — lives in Chatswood with the barbecue chickens.' I went on to try and describe the kind of restaurant that hangs ducks upside down in its front window, an image that had fluttered into my mind and seemed impossibly amusing at that moment, definitely one for sharing. The funny thing about nitrous oxide (if you've had it, you know there's only like a *million* funny things about nitrous oxide) is that you sober up the second you stop breathing it in. Because I had to keep still during the epidural, the nurse wrestled the Milo tube out of my hand and I was instantly, painfully, lucid.

'Oh, um, sorry about the chickens thing.' I smiled weakly at my hard-working doctor. He smiled back and said he would take my observations as a compliment. Those ducks *are* pretty funny.

I had been in labour for only a couple of hours when the epidural went in, and all that time, nobody had taken more than a fleeting visit downtown. Dilation is supposed to take forever when you're induced, so no need, they thought — but after thirty minutes of my numb-spinery, a midwife with nothing to do decided to take a look-see. Get the lie of the land, as it were.

'Oh my God, the head's out!' she shouted, holding my sheet aloft like someone who has just opened the door of their tent and found a tiger cub inside. Apparently the baby had started out on her own. I burst out laughing.

'No! Don't laugh!' the midwife shouted. 'You'll laugh the baby out and I haven't got anything ready. I need my trolley.'

To have a baby without noticing — that is a gift that only the young and exceptionally loose of pelvis can hope for in this life, but reader, I was *that* loose. As soon as a little team assembled,

I gave one teensy push and an even teensier baby, glistening and purple, was scooped out. Bitsy.

Minky had been adamant the entire pregnancy that we call the baby Courtney-Dawnie, irrespective of gender. While we mulled that and other possibilities, we stuck with Bitsy. Bitsy and Minky. The girls, the children. One of the first, funnest things about having a second baby is choosing a collective term for your pair. It's so grown-up and parenty saying 'the kids', 'the children', 'the little ones' or whatever you settle on. I know of somebody who calls her two the mittens; Lizzie calls hers the smallwins. I liked that; I thought I might use that. Then, before anything had a chance to stick, I accidentally called my pair 'the nerds' and it stuck hard.

'I can't,' I'll say to Shab about something, 'I have to go pick up the nerds.'

'How are the nerds? All right?' he'll call and ask around lunch time most days.

I held the newest nerd in my arms. She squalled and writhed, incensed by the whole business of birth. This child was angry. If a doctor had even needed to smack her to elicit a first cry, there's a realistic chance she would have smacked him back. She was beautiful and strong and from the get-go, as funny as I'd know, but this three kilos of undiluted rage was, over the next two years, going to take her entire family to the absolute brink. I thought we'd been there already but Bitsy had in mind an even brinkier spot for us to set up camp. She would make Shab and I more bewildered, frustrated and wild with despair than we'd ever been. She would make us both mad with fatigue. She would win over every stranger she met, while making her own mother wonder if all that talk about loving your second just like your first was rubbish. Whereas Minky made me feel like the glowingest of good mothers, Bitsy made me feel beaten and clueless from about three days in. Oh, but I loved her. It wouldn't matter what she did, how defiant she could be, how maddeningly contrary. She was mine and I loved her every bit as hardly as the first.

Two years later, I would find Bitsy in the kitchen, sitting at the table with a row of peaches in front of her, every one with a perfect round bite out of the side. I know that any child-antic story that starts with 'I found x in the x' is, bottom line, your fault because you weren't there supervising when the game got started. Every anecdote my mother has about my brother and I starts with 'So, I found you ...' So, I found you cutting your brother's hair; I found you both in the dryer; I found you up at the shops. I honestly think we were lost to her most of the time, and just every now and again a burning smell would prompt her to come look for us. So, I found Bitsy in the kitchen with all these half-eaten peaches. And I was cross because when you sign up to become a mother on a budget, what you're really signing up for is a decade-long bout of scurvy. 'No, I shouldn't,' I will think, returning an orange to the fruit bowl. 'I should save it for the children. It's more important that they have it.' It's the same instinctive thinking that causes starving mother lions to hang back and watch their wuzzy little cubs eat fresh gazelle to the point of bellyache while their own skeletal haunches all but burst through their mangy pelts. To eat a blueberry with impunity, I have to wait until it has been licked, dropped, rolled in sand and ultimately rejected by the more important mini-human I bought it for. Even an apple has to make a round trip to preschool in a humid lunchbox before I can eat it without gagging from guilt. Which explains why I have once or twice held up a half-eaten punnet of strawberries, only the pointy ends bitten off, and shouted, 'Nerds, these things are the *diamonds* of the fruit world; you can't *waste* them!' while the children look at me like they can hear lambs screaming inside my head. Bitsy's peaches stunt, then, I unsurprisingly found irksome.

'Right, Bits,' I said, 'you're going to sit there and finish one whole peach.' I thought about making her eat them all, like people do when they find their teenagers smoking, but that would surely mean more cleaning up for me, and I'm always after less.

'Don't want to,' Bitsy said, rolling over onto her tummy to climb down backwards from her chair.

'Too bad. You started them all, so you're going to finish one. Call me when you're done,' I said, piling up the rest of the peaches in my arm and putting them back in the fridge.

'Finished,' she said an unfeasibly short time later.

'Bitsy, I can see it under your chair.'

'Finished,' she said again in 30 more seconds.

'Bitsy, seriously. I'm not dumb. I can see the peach in your pants.'

'OK, well, I go eat it in da gardin,' she said, ambling outside.

A minute or so later, because I had learned to distrust her so deeply, I went outside to check her progress. I figured she was burying the peach or trying to throw it over the fence. But no, there she was, holding open our rabbit's hutch, leaning in so far that her feet were nearly off the ground, and rolling the now skinless fruit around in the particular corner that Snowflake had chosen for his commode.

'Bitsy! Stop!' I said, picking her up under the arms.

'Nwah, can't eat it now, Mummy, peeeesh all dirty,' she said as though something really sad had just happened to her. She opened her hand, dropped the peach on the ground, and I carried her back inside, a few more points down.

That was later. Right then in the hospital, I breathed in her smell, stroked her tiny, fuzzy forearms, which were so soft I could barely feel them. I held her until my arms ached and promised her I'd do my best. Then I discharged us early and went home via Woolworths just in case there was any kind of prize on offer for being a total martyr.

10

INSUFFICIENT FUNDS

I HAVE A STRANGE RELATIONSHIP WITH MONEY. I LIKE IT very much, but I don't have any of it. As much as anything else — sleep deprivation or unidentifiable stains on my clothing — money defined the first years post-Minky and became a permanent red alert post-Bitsy. Before we had children, I never thought about money because I had it. A journalist's salary is never particularly shiny until your photo is above your writing, but Shab's was, and there was nothing to spend either wage on except restaurant food and weekends in Nice. After Minky, Shab's salary was still good, only now there were three people living on it.

When a couple sits down and tries to work out whether they can afford a child (I have heard that people do that), they usually tot up the cost of a car seat, a cot and a stroller with disc brakes. But no already-struggling parent would lose a moment's sleep over those things. You can avoid buying them altogether if you're willing to borrow, improvise or hold on to the handle of a cheap Valco really tightly when you're walking down a hill. What you can't avoid paying for, what makes parents weep every time they walk through the sensor doors of any retail outlet, is the wipes, the nappies, the food, the clothing, the sodium lauryl sulphate–free bath wash, the toys, books and the $24 sippy cups, which are designed to drop silently out of the stroller the minute you leave home. And unlike those one-off purchases from Babies 'N' Things, the essentials need to be restocked roughly every ten days. Once I stopped working, Minky was born and my lavish government maternity pay of 60 whole pounds a fortnight ceased, I had to learn to be careful with money. There are three reasons why that would be difficult. Two are definitely my dumb fault; one is not.

First, I had never had to be careful with money before, not once, so I didn't know how to go without something I wanted, buy a cheaper version of it or even, truth be told, check the price of something before I took it to the counter. Getting halfway through your twenties without learning that is shameful. As with most of my myriad shortcomings, I blame my parents.

They're bailers, always have been. Between the ages of 0 and 22, my parents bailed me out of every slightly difficult or totally disastrous situation I found myself in, especially fiscal ones. Once, as a teenager, I asked to borrow my father's brand-new laptop, which, because it was 1993, was the same weight and thickness as two reams of A3 paper stacked one on the other. It cost him probably $16,000. I took it to my room, messed around for a while on the cutting-edge SuperPaint program, then went up the street for a Calippo. I had been out for 30 minutes or so when the sky turned dark grey and it began to rain in a very monsoony way. When I got home, I went up to my room and saw that I had left the laptop by an open window, where it was now sitting in a pool of rainwater.

'No, no, no, no, no,' I cried, as I skittered over to see if there was any possible way I hadn't destroyed it. I picked it up and a torrent of water spilled out from underneath. The screen had gone completely black except for half of a flickering arrow and an ampersand. I started to shake. My father would be home in a few hours, and even though he isn't a fearful figure, he was a passionate early adopter who would feel understandably dismayed that his thoughtless daughter had drowned a major tech purchase. I wailed for three whole hours while I waited for him to come home, simultaneously hairdryering the screen, inserting wadded tissues into the disk drive and sucking water out from in between the keys with a drinking straw. Later, as I tried to extract disintegrated tissues from the disk drive with a fork, I heard keys in the door. I ran straight downstairs with the computer in my hands, no mean feat since it began life at ten kilos and was now carrying the same in water weight.

'Dad, I'm so sorry, I'm so sorry, I've done something terrible. I'm so sorry,' I cried.

'Calm down, darling. Are you OK? What's happened?' he said.

'I leftaaaaah … your computeraaaaah … in the rain and it's ruinedaaaaah,' I said, sobbing with renewed vigour.

'Did you do it on purpose?' he asked calmly, as though I was a lovable toddler who'd just drawn on the wall, rather than a stupid teen who couldn't shut a window.

'No,' I said, wiping my nose on the sleeve of my DKNY hoodie.

'You all right?' he asked.

'Yes,' I said, bewildered.

'You look like you're fairly sorry.'

'I am.'

'Well then, I don't think we've got anything to worry about here,' he said, lifting the laptop out of my arms and pretending not to notice as a final trickle of rain soaked the front of his suit trousers. I was always bailed out, reason one why being careful with money was going to be difficult.

The second reason: buying things makes me happy, sometimes for as long as 15 minutes. It always has, but once there was a baby and nothing in the diary, the happy distraction that a purchase has always been to me was intensified. The other day Snooch popped over. She sat beside Minky while she counted out her collection of five-cent pieces, buttons, foreign coins and play money, listing all the things she was saving up for. 'Buying things doesn't make you happy, Tiny,' said Snooch. A split second later, they both burst out laughing. 'Of course it does, Minky, I'm just being silly. Buying things is brilliant!' Buying things *is* brilliant, and if you've been a stay-at-homer for a week or more, you already know that buying things is an excellent salve to an otherwise ordinary day. It is something to do, somewhere to go, and provides a little zip of excitement when the bag gets handed over. And if, even better, you get home and the purchase turns out to be lame and needs exchanging, well, there's something to do tomorrow as well.

I couldn't go just anywhere and transact, though. I had to go to nice places. Schlepping to the Mothercare on the Hammersmith King Street, a stretch of retail that makes North End Road look like the Rue Saint-Honoré, made me feel grim and tacky, and tainted the purchase even after I got it home. So when I had to buy something already a bit ordinary, like nappy cream or a packet of tiny flannels, I shopped at places where my purchase would be wrapped in tissue and handed over in a thick, ribbon-handled bag — the baby department of Peter Jones, Daisy & Tom on the King's Road, or Selfridges if I was in the neighbourhood. It was a much more enjoyable experience then, even if it meant that I routinely paid 20 per cent extra for staples, a sort of voluntary pleasantness levy. The mothers who could genuinely afford to shop in those places usually had cars with drivers waiting outside, but I would happily spend £9.50 for an infant toothbrush so I could mingle with them, instead of the mothers at Putney Superdrug, who would threaten to take their baby's Happy Meal away if it didn't stop crying. This is another of my less excusable personality traits, but there you have it. There were other supposed 'living costs' associated with being a 25-year-old stay-at-home mother in London that I was equally wanton about and not the least bit sorry for. I let myself spend as much as I wanted on parking, no questions asked. I would not stop buying £5 coffees multiple times a day, and I was always going to buy flowers the day after pay, because those things made me feel better and, over time, would work out cheaper than electroshock therapy and a spell in The Priory, which I felt sure was the alternative.

Stay-at-homers are also constantly in harm's way, retail wise, the third reason why that particular life phase was a sub-optimal time to try and learn budgeting. When you're shut up in an office all day, the only things to buy, really, are hot beverages, rail cards and, if it's raining at lunch time, discounted Pedro Garcias from theoutnet.com. That's never going to break the bank, especially since you're at work at the time and therefore

actually earning money while you sit and click through Garcia's
A/W colourways. On the other hand, when you're at a semi-
loose end every hour of every day, there is so much to buy:
magazines, Boost Juices, lip balm, books, coffee, packet ravioli,
Moleskine notebooks, Moleskine diaries, Moleskine combined
diary–notebooks, BPA-free drink bottles and a stupid toy that
your child gets attached to in the chemist. That's all before
you've even got home and opened your laptop. Even though I
banned myself from daytime website perusal in my early rallying
days, I didn't extend the embargo to e-commerce, since online
shopping could be classified as a legitimate nap-time PAM
(personal administration matter). And, gosh, there are so many
excellent things for sale inside computers. With a growing baby,
there's always something you can justify buying, even if it's only
fresh bath toys because the other ones got that crazy black stuff
inside and when you squirted water out of the whale's mouth
last time, your baby got coated with sludgy mould flakes. As
your child gets older, buying things *for* them — treats, bribes,
consolations — feels like an excellent way to cancel out low-
quality parenting and is something for the two of you to enjoy
together in lieu of talking. It never ends.

But it had to. For me, anyway. When Minky was eight
months old, Shab came home from work one day at 11.30 a.m.
'Always for dinner, never for lunch' is a rule I like to live by
where husbands are concerned. Their being home in the middle

of the day usually indicates that something is not as it should be: they are sick, you wigged out at the baby and made them come home early to sub you off, or, as in this instance, they just got canned. If never again I have to see my life partner stumble through the front door with a box of workplace accoutrement in his arms, I will die a happy woman.

Right then, as Shab collapsed onto the sofa and explained the why and what-the-what of the company-wide shut down that had just gone over, I thought about our bank account and wondered what exactly we were going to do. We had a few hundred pounds in savings but otherwise we were high-end hand-to-mouthing it, true mid-twenties style. Neither set of parents was in a spot to bail us out to the required degree, so apart from a month's severance, we were sans safety net. We had known, in a far-off way, that redundancy might happen — the tech bubble was now just a sticky patch on the floor of the LSE — but we were hoping to sell up and leave London before it did. We would leave eventually, but there would be some gruelling, payday-less months before then. The days of profligate spending were over, for good.

I'm sure there are women — I've seen them, actually, walking around Harvey Nichols with armloads of Versace children's wear, the swing tags tangling up like Christmas lights — who never get close to the rocky bottom of their bank accounts. I can't imagine what that is like any more. They probably buy blueberries when they're £7 a punnet and care less when their toddler throws them all over the floor of the car. And I bet they fill up that car with that really treaty petrol on purpose, not because they grabbed the wrong hose. Once I might have been the same, but after having a baby and dropping from two incomes, to one, to none, exigencies of that sort faded from my memory like old Polaroids. Later, when Bitsy was born and the salary-to-dependant ratio in our house ratcheted up to an almost unfeasible 1:4, Shab's income began to feel like genuine starvation rations instead of the decent pay cheque it actually was. Four whole humans were dipping into it daily for clothes, food, rent, preschool fees, Nurofen (regular and infant) and other essentials. One Sunday night, after the children were in bed, Shab flicked the television on to a nature documentary. 'Adult polar bears,' the narrator explained, 'can ordinarily survive by making a kill once every three weeks, but now with two hungry cubs to feed, this bear must make a kill every single day.'

'True *dat*,' he said, before switching over to a 'Friends' repeat because it felt like less pressure.

The financial strain that we were under now, every day except for the one directly after payday, began to feel like two hands around my neck. Trying to be careful where possible became instead a constant, dreadful obsession with money. A parking ticket would send me into a paroxysm of despair; a lost $10 note would have me scrabbling around in my bag like a desperate

179

smoker searching for a lighter after a long-haul flight. A bag of carrots turning flopsy in the fridge before I used them would incite a half-day of bitter self-reproach. I became adept at acting surprised when my card got declined in a store ('Ha! That's odd. It just worked next door ...') and christened the first day of the week 'No Fruit Monday' because it meant exactly that after a weekend of debauched apple eating by Minky. There wouldn't be fresh supplies until Wednesday, grocery day, so if the fruit situation got dire in the first half of the week and I began to worry about vitamin deficiency and brain development, I would take us all to the supermarket at 5 p.m. and throw what I like to call a 'Woolworths Buffet'. More principled people would call it 'Stealing', but either way, it meant spending a protracted period in the supermarket and encouraging the under-fives to eat as much loose produce as possible without drawing attention to themselves.

Penury also meant, of course, that there could be no luxuries, no baby-sitters, cleaning ladies or expensive maternity nurses to help out with newborn Bitsy in lieu of a grandparent, nothing that could cushion some of each day's hard graft. Any sanity-sustaining treats had to go. Before, austerity meant saying 'Tap's fine' in a restaurant; now it meant walking right by that restaurant and home to a glass of Brita and some seaweed crackers. I heard a song at the time by Nina Simone, or Mona Sanine if you're Minky and a bit hard-up in the pronunciation department. It became a jaunty anthem for me in the days of our post-Bitsy privation. I would include the lyrics, but I'm pretty sure if you put a song in your book you have to pay for it, and scrimping is muscle memory to me now. In it, Sanine lists all the things she doesn't have — culture, skirts, beer, a home, perfume, friends, schooling, shoes or a mother. And then halfway through, she flips and lists everything she does have — her hands, her brain, her smile, her chin, her neck, her sex, her boobies.

I didn't have premium denim, enough fruit or, three days out of seven, credit on my phone, but I did have my chin, neck and boobies. I was breast-feeding again, so actually I had a tonne of boobies. I had life, freedom, my brains, my heart. I also had two perfectly healthy children and a kind husband who was doing his darnedest, and whether or not it sounds like a supersize cliché, I needed to stop looking at all the ways in which we were deficient, stop feeling like we'd messed up and were being punished, and get on with it. The whole 'starving children in Africa' bit has never worked on me the way it should. Thinking about those worse off than me has never made me feel better about my life's comparative bounty when there is somebody right next to me in the newsagent getting the UK *Elle* and *Vanity Fair* and I have to choose between them or, in especially lean times, swing by a medical centre and read staphylococcal-crusted back issues instead. What did work for me and make all this First-World hardship pay for itself was remembering that this was all a choice. Our whole life, as it was, was my idea. I had chosen to have children, albeit without a bunch of due diligence. I had chosen to give up my job and stay at home with them. Perhaps if I'd dropped them into childcare and gone back to work, we would have had more money. I chose not to. Even though it was tiring and often more depressing than a Centrelink queue, it was a good choice and it meant something. When a woman at playgroup asked me if I 'owned, or … ?' I would force myself to remember that I was renting because doing so meant I could be home. Maybe we could have bought the house I wanted so badly in Sydney if I'd been willing to sacrifice the intangible wealth that is sitting on a spot of sunny grass watching your two babies tussle over a Vita-Weat. But I wasn't.

Having a system also helped. Don't panic! I'm not about to copy and paste my budgeting spreadsheet onto the page. I don't even know how to make those boxes add up in Excel, so we're OK there, take a breath. A system, I mean, that infused my financial situ with a little dignity. Once I was at home, I was living — no matter how I iced it — on somebody else's money. The husbands of stay-at-homers fail them in many ways but one of the most timeworn is by making them feel like they're on a short fiscal leash. Nobody should ever have to answer this question just after her husband logs on to anz.com: 'What did you spend fifty-seven dollars on at Bed, Bath N' Table?' That would be humiliating, and even if she could remember, it's probably dirty or broken by now.

Like every woman who signs up for the giant self-esteem-depletion experiment that is full-time housewifery, I needed access to funds that were just mine, and complete autonomy over them, even though somebody else earned them and they were only a twenty and change. The day I realised that, I went and opened a new bank account. I have heard that other women call it Running Away Money. With the balance of my Running Away account I could have got maybe three kilometres in a cab off peak, but the point was, it was private, I managed it myself and it was always there, so I never had to ask Shab for money in that most Betty Draperish 'Can I have some cash?' kind of way. The account is still in use all this time later, and although the balance will assuredly drop into the single figures at the end of every month, nobody in our house feels like a character from *The Women's Room*. Win!

I never believed it when anyone told me that the lean years would eventually end. It is like someone telling me that my children won't need therapy when they're adults — a nice idea but impossible to believe. I couldn't see how we'd ever move on from here. After bringing my adrenal system to the point of collapse over the price of comestibles, I couldn't imagine ever slinging a tray of organic cutlets into the trolley without a second thought. I don't want to spoil the ending, but I also don't want you to throw yourself under an oncoming people mover because nobody told you the money famine eventually breaks. It does — but I, we, everybody has to wait.

11

BONUS GRANNY

GENERALLY SPEAKING, I DON'T CARE FOR THIS SENTENCE: 'IF there's anything I can do to help, just call me.' It's usually meant kindly, but right out of the gate, I have a job to do. I have to place a call. And very likely at the end of that call, I'll have to digest a meaty gobbet of disappointment because, as it turns out, they're actually pretty tied up. I'll feel presumptuous for even asking and exhausted from the emotional prep that went into ringing in the first place. Plus, what if the sort of help they had in mind was posting a letter for me, and I call to ask if they'll be my doula? It's a minefield, so whenever the offer is made, I routinely ignore it.

A few weeks after we moved back to Australia, I got a call from the mother of one of Shab's old school friends, a lady in her early sixties. I'd met her at our wedding and a few other

185

times, and I liked her quite a bit. She'd heard that we were back in Sydney with a child, and because she knew we had no family about, we should let her know, she said, if we ever needed a baby-sitter. I thanked her heartily, said I definitely would and hung up the phone knowing I absolutely wouldn't.

A little while later, she called again. She wondered if Minky and I had time to pop in for a cup of tea and a play in her garden. Did we have time? Let me see. I scanned my diary, which, except for a ten-minute vaccination appointment in early May, was mostly blank. It looked like an adolescent's diary, when there are pages and pages and pages of nothing, then ***MY BIRTHDAY!!!!!**** and nothing else until Christmas. Since it was an invitation for tea and not an offer of baby-sitting, I also needn't worry that I'd have to pay her back somehow. I'm a terrible reciprocator. Not because I don't try — I try too hard. I have no sense of balance, so if ever another mother minds the girls for an hour, I will have to buy her children ponies and take them all skiing.

Mrs McCarron, as Shab still called her, so I did too, lived in a wooden cottage, painted appley green. It was on a quiet street in a particularly leafy North Shore suburb, where it is not unusual for people to own their own grass. Unlike the nouveau couples moving in latterly to raise four-child status families, Mrs McCarron was born there, and, to this day, I'm not convinced that she has spent more than two consecutive nights in another postcode. She told us to come down the side;

she would be in the garden, she said. And on the appointed day Minky and I did just that. The garden was deep and green and dappled. It was perfectly tended in that way only grannies' gardens are, with flowers and lemon trees instead of a clinical row of yuccas along the side of a stupid lap pool. There was a pond and an almost greedy abundance of butterflies and bright pink fuchsias, which Mrs McCarron showed Minky how to pick and turn into ballerinas by threading one of the stamens through the body. A little while after we arrived, Minky was sitting on a blanket in the shade dancing a ballerina in each hand, and Mrs McCarron went inside and came out with a tray of tea and shortbread, a lemon cake, and a bowl of fruit and toffee popcorn for Minky. I wanted to stay forever.

Mrs McCarron nattered to me about people I didn't know as though we were all intimates: who had another grandchild on the way, who was downsizing, who had just booked an 18-night culture cruise through the canals of Northern Europe. I listened peacefully, like you do to background radio while you're cooking. After an hour more, I snapped to and wondered if we had stayed too long, but Mrs McCarron insisted not. She hadn't even got out the box of faded wooden toys that the best grannies keep on hand for visiting children, and she had lunch ready for us too when we got hungry again. We stayed until the last possible minute before Minky's afternoon sleep and left with a shallow cardboard box full of herbs, cut flowers and

English spinach, as well as the rest of the lemon cake wrapped in a tea towel. She waved goodbye from the footpath, another visit already penned onto her calendar ('English Country Houses', 2005). As we pulled away from the kerb, a deeply satiated Minky asked from the car seat, 'Dat one of mine?'

'Is what one of yours?'

'Dat granny.'

Oh, right. 'No, not really,' I said, not sure whom to be saddest for. 'But I suppose she's like a bonus granny, an extra one since ours are all away.'

''K,' said Minky, happy with that. 'Bonus granny.'

The very best thing about a bonus granny, as opposed to the real thing, is that the emotional terrain between you is entirely untreacherous. Real grandmothers are, after all, either your mother or mother-in-law, so the chances of you feeling uncomplicatedly grateful towards them or happy in their company are slim. After a few visits, Mrs McCarron asked if I'd like to leave Minky sometimes and go up to the nearby café and read my book, for a break. I did, and felt grateful but not indebted or accused in some passive-aggressive way of 'not managing', like I might have if my own mother had offered the same. I didn't really care if Mrs McCarron fed Minky the wrong things or let her miss a sleep, because she wasn't contradicting my instructions on purpose like real grannies do for kicks. There's nothing a real granny loves more, apparently, than waiting for her daughter to leave, then chain-feeding the baby sweets, because all these modern mothers are so precious about their children's diets and need to be shown that a bit of lovely sugar never hurt anyone. I never felt judged or second-guessed or even observed by Mrs McCarron; I just felt at rest. Her old-fashioned habits, like answering the landline and using a travel agent, didn't bother me in the least, although I bet they drove her own children crazy. Sometimes I'd try and parse her reason for being so kind to me for no reward. Apart from the fact she was just nice and did things like that, I'd wonder if perhaps she enjoyed a grandparentish exchange without any subtext, atmosphere or refreshing of old wounds. Maybe it is liberating to feed a two-year-old a Fantale without risking a bitter reiteration of your many failings as mother and grandmother.

Still, there is a different emotion that can trip you up with a bonus granny, and it's jealousy. Much later, after dozens more visits like that, we popped in to Mrs McCarron's one day, to find another little girl in the garden, the daughter of a neighbour who'd gone to do jobs. Minky was furious. She sulked from start to finish and guarded the best fuchsia bush like it was the last of that species. She was jealous. I understood; I felt exactly the same. Mrs McCarron was *our* fake granny and I wanted that other little princess to split. Mrs McCarron had real grandchildren of her own but they lived hours away, in the country. She talked about them occasionally, and I was always interested to hear updates, although grateful that she didn't go *on* about them. And even more grateful when, our first Christmas back in Australia, she gave Minky an Advent calendar that had her name on it. She picked it out of a pile of Advent calendars that were inscribed for each of her real grandchildren. She had folded us in and I was so thankful. And so jealous.

My envy came in a wider, more generic strain too. I spent a large slice of each day coveting any other granny, not just Mrs McCarron. The certain-age women I'd see pushing strollers and swings or assisting on supermarket expeditions like obedient Sherpas — I yearned for them; I pined. I checked out other grannies in the street like men check out ladies. If we happened to be somewhere that older women congregate, like on the footpath outside an Art Deco cinema that does combined movie and light lunch deals at 11 a.m., I'd pick my favourite. I am not proud about it, but I know for a fact I'm not the only one who does it. Soon I would meet a new friend, another motherless mother, who does the same thing. As it happens, she goes for the real Blythe Danner types — tall, slender older ladies with fawny-grey bobs. I like my grannies conservative. Slacks, fob chains, a short perm; I'd take a hand-knitted cardigan if one was on offer. Our taste in fake grannies was the only thing my new friend and I wouldn't have in common. In every other way, we would be soul mates, doppelgängers, sisters from another mister. OK, *fine*, taste in fake grannies and only one of us used to be a model.

12

THE MILTTT

AT THREE, MINKY REACHED AN IMPORTANT DEVELOPMENTAL milestone that comes just after speaking in full sentences and non-maiming use of cutlery. She became an obsessive hoarder. Any object could arouse her possessive instinct — a one-legged Polly Pocket, a broken hairclip we found in the park — but her mania was centred on a series of collectable princess figurines, and whenever we walked past a toyshop that sold them, and I was sure my card would work, we added another one to her number.

'I'm missing one still, Mummy,' Minky said, kneeling on her bed and lining her collection up along the windowsill one afternoon.

'Which one?' I asked.

'I don't know,' she answered, 'but shall we go to the shops?' It was a three-year-old's way of saying 'I'll know it when I see it.'

Sometimes you don't know who is missing from your set until you see them. There was, I thought as Minky and I walked hand in hand to the shop, still one figure missing from my collection of non-plastic people. I had the prince, two limited edition babies, my favourite Girl-Shab, a lovely pair of fairy godmothers in Snooch and Bonus Granny, and enough random princesses to get a good game going, but still, no main heroine. The one I could take everywhere with me, tucked in my pocket, for constant reassurance and company. We would spend so much time together, I imagined, we'd create our own language, like Nell in the movie *Nell*. All 'Tay ina win', all the time. It was really my dream, since, although I was nearly four years into my maternal exchange program, I still ran into language problems on a daily basis. I could speak fluent Toily when I needed to, but I never *wanted* to — I longed to talk about my own topics in my own language with someone else who innately understood.

Right before Bitsy was born, we had moved into a little apartment that sat on the top floor of a two-storey building from the 1920s. From the outside it looked like a decommissioned mental asylum but inside it was freshly painted and light, with sash windows on every side. It was a peaceful, quiet haven, with a view over trees and terracotta rooftops. There was a playground directly across the street, set in a circle of tall poplar trees. On the other side of the park, there was a double-fronted cottage, painted lemon, with roses climbing over the front door. While it was still just Minky and I, Bitsy tucked away in utero, we majored in variety where daily outings were concerned, rarely visiting the same park twice, in an effort to sidestep that sense of daytime déjà vu a mother gets when she straps the same child into the same swing in the same outfit at the same time of day, five days in a row. Once there was Bitsy and a capsule or a stroller and a bag of babycrap, the idea of getting in the car and driving to a new playground every day post-nap was too overwhelming, so I gave up just a little and started going to the one across the street most afternoons. The path of least equipment and all.

Visiting the same park every day can mean falling in with a group of other regulars. Sometimes those regulars turn out to be kindreds; sometimes they turn out to be totally unintelligible mummy-foreigners who can only be understood with a lot of awkwardness and gesticulation. It's impossible to tell who's who until you start trying to converse. I don't remember the name of the first regular I hooked up with there, since she'd kind of outshone herself in the name department by calling her baby daughter Persephone ('It's pronounced Per-sef-any, you know, like Stephanie but heaps nicer'). She was heavily into astrology and would ask every mother she met when their child was born, so that any quality it then displayed, like listlessness or whining, could be put down to it being 'such a Libran' or 'your typical Aries'. Speaking personally on behalf of myself, I think astrology is a wee bit bogus. How can a person's entire personality be explained by their birth date? The only question your birth date answers is 'When did my parents pants each other?' and I don't want to know the answer to that. If counting nine months backwards doesn't land you on Dad's birthday, let's assume he got a pay rise somewhere in there and move on, is what I think.

Persephone's mother did not feel the same, and whenever we crossed over at the park, we battled gamely through a conversation about the dark arts and/or her partner's lazy sperm. She was desperate to conceive a second time, but there were a number of obstacles or 'misalignments' in her way, she told me, the lazy sperm chief amongst them. Her partner didn't have a job either and was often seen walking to and from the corner shop during the day with a Discman balanced on his flat palm (remember how you couldn't put a Discman sideways in your pocket because the CD inside would jump? — that) staring into the middle distance, stooped of shoulder, a little spent looking. She was also nearly 40 and she felt that her eggs were 'on the turn', she said, as I winced into the cup of tea I'd carried over from home. On top of her shrivelling ovaries and her partner's failure to contribute financially or procreatively was the even more pressing issue of timing. If she didn't conceive before February, they were going to have to take a month-long break from all the rumping because 'no way' was she 'having another Scorpio'. I nodded in forced sympathy and tried to break eye contact in a way that might discourage her from plying me with any additional detail. I fixed my gaze instead on the lemon-coloured cottage over the way.

At the same moment, the front door opened and out walked a tall, pale redhead with an angelic blonde baby who looked about ten months old, the same age as Bitsy, hoisted upon her model-skinny hip. I watched as she bounced a bugaboo down the steps, collapsed it and flung it into the boot of her car with one lithesome shake of her wrist. Me holding a baby, wrenching open the car boot and trying to dominate a stubborn stroller tended to involve the full ass up, flailing limbs, dropped bag, spilt wallet, exposure of my soft, mumsy haunches, panting, the smoothing of hair, the pulling down of T-shirt. Just looking at her made me feel like the big Kardashian.

It wouldn't take. She was a stone-cold MILTTT (Mother I'd Like To Talk To). She started coming to the park with the baby every afternoon from then on, and she just seemed too pleasant and interesting, always chatting amiably to whatever lonely housewife latched on to her, appearing absorbed by their bullshit-bullshit anecdotes. Every day I tried to hot up my jealous feelings towards her roses, her modelly body and her perfectly dishabille ensembles (how many blousons can one person own? I used to wonder) into proper antagonism, but I couldn't make it happen. I'd rather chat. For two whole months, I did nothing about it except steal sideways glances at her while she was looking the other way, because no-one likes to be caught staring at another woman with their mouth a bit open.

Then Shab went back to London for a two-week work trip, and Minky and Bitsy caught hand, foot and mouth disease, a highly contagious childhood special that presents as a lot of little blisters on the hands, feet and, if memory serves, mouth. It kept the three of us inside, solely and unrelentingly in each other's company, 24 hours a day, for an entire week. By the time the nerds recovered and we could venture outside, I was so hard-up for adult conversation I would have agreed on the spot to a mini-break with Double Denifer had she been there to offer it. We unlatched the park gate, our first afternoon out, and I saw the redhead pushing her daughter on the swings. I ambled towards her, still not sure if I had the wherewithal to start the conversation but motivated powerfully by cabin fever. As I turned around to work out an exit strategy, I saw Persephone and her mother tussling with the gate behind me. Either I engaged with the redhead right now or my afternoon would be three rounds with that classic Virgo on conception by the stars.

'HELLO!' I just said it. Not clever, and maybe a little loud as well. Oh, hang on, I'm still talking. 'HOW ARE YOU?

I'M MEG MASON.' Wow, surname too, that's odd. Nerves, I guess. Either way, it was done.

'Hi! Good, thanks,' the redhead said, lighting up in a way that made me think she had been working up to an introduction too. 'I'm Nona … Marsh. Do you think I have Bunny in backwards?'

She did; she did have her daughter in the bucket swing backwards, so that the child was forced to adopt the position of a pre-ripcord skydiver. After she extracted Bunny from the swing, I introduced the nerds and we rafted up our rugs and sat on the grass for a bit.

'How's your week going?' Nona asked.

'Oh well, my husband's away and it's all getting a bit Plathy at ours,' I answered, forgetting to translate my private term for a not-very-happy, Sylvia Plath–style crawl-under-the-house sort of day into mum-friendly English.

'Oh, I've just read *The Bell Jar* again. It's just as perfect as toast, isn't it?' Nona sighed, passing out Ritz crackers to Bunny, then Bitsy and Minky. I'd never heard anyone use 'as toast' as a superlative before, but I knew what she meant.

'Have a Rit, Minky,' she said. 'They're a poor man's Jat.'

'That's funny,' I said. 'I was just telling my mother on the phone this morning how MAC is a poor man's NARS.'

'Ta,' Minky said.

'Oh no, darling,' I said, as a reflex, 'We don't say "ta" in this family.'

'Ooooh, we're ta-haters too,' Nona said. 'Thin end of the wedge, I think. Next you'll be eating bickies on the poddy. Not PLU.'

'People …' I guessed.

'Like Us.'

'TAY INA WIN!! TAY INA WIN!!' I wanted to shout. Someone who spoke my language! I had found her. I felt like an American stumbling across an open McDonald's while lost in downtown Karachi. Had I dreamed her up? I suddenly wondered. No, because if I'd invented her, I would have made her fatter than me. She must be real. An hour or so later we were still sitting cross-legged on the grass, comparing notes from our time at home.

'What is with "Good swinging"?' Nona said. 'Have you heard that?'

'Totally,' I said. 'It's a bit bonkers, isn't it, complimenting your child for gravity?'

'And all the "mate" business,' she replied.

'Oh, like "Mate, mate, come on, stop hitting Dad"?' I asked.

'Exactly.' Nona laughed. '"Come on, mate, stand up. Mate, you're stretching my T-shirt."'

'Why are you laughing so hardly?' Minky shouted from the swings. Because, having never met until now, Nona and I just had so much to catch up on. Eventually we broke up for the afternoon and went home. Nona had put my number into her phone, and later that night as I was Pine-o-Cleening

Bolognese off the wall, my phone pipped. 'Have not laughed that hardly since Persephone puked in the spinny teacup. Hope bed, bath and table goes fastly for the Masonettes tonight. See you tomorrow.'

I knew I *would* see her tomorrow — I already saw her every day, since we were neighbours and all — but the really exciting thing was, now I could look forward to talking to her out loud and not just in my head. Thinking up interesting questions and the other person's responses gets quite tiring.

Over time we shared the entire back catalogue of our children's best linguistic mishaps and folded them all into a new, shared vernacular that filled the toily vacuum: 'hardly', 'so much jobs'; Minky thinking the magazine shop is the 'News-Asian' and describing herself as 'hungry for drinking' when she meant thirsty; Bitsy's first word, 'dong-dongs', which meant but in no way sounded like 'sausage'. Bunny thought soy protein was called toe-food; Bitsy was sure she had ear-loafs. Minky was introduced to both hummus and 'Thomas the Tank Engine' in the same week, and they became fatally confused, so that we all ate Thomas and crackers while watching 'Hummus the Tank Engine' from then on. Bunny coined the term 'playgroot' and we all started describing anything undesirable as 'a bit grooted'. We collected more as we went along.

One afternoon, we were all in the park chatting to a clutch of regulars. A mother in the circle was trying desperately to steer the conversation in her direction. She clearly had a corking anecdote saved up but couldn't find a natural entrée. Eventually she lost patience, and as another woman rounded out her story, the desperate mother wrenched the conversation her way with a bold: 'That's funny. Actually, *speaking* of anecdotes …' I smiled and looked over at Nona, whose eyes had widened almost imperceptibly. She knew what I meant. Sometimes a common language means not needing to say a word.

Anyway, *speaking* of anecdotes, Nona, Bunny, Bitsy, Minky and I soon started venturing beyond our shared park, which became known as home base, base camp, the bark park or the BPG. We booked in for the same swimming class so that we could sit and chat while the girls did their supervised drowning work. One week, as we both clapped absent-mindedly at Minky's best dive — 'No, that wasn't it! Watch! That wasn't it either.' — Bonus Granny arrived at the pool with her grandson who was visiting from the country. Usually, seeing Bonus Granny with her real grandchildren made me feel misty with envy and displacement. This time, it didn't. I made introductions, and as the three of us sat and chatted, my mind flittered back to my desperate bid to befriend the reluctant Swede. I had, I realised suddenly, a very full set of real-life figurines, and here they were, lined up along the pool deck nattering so hardly. I had what I had always wanted. Finally, a complete collection.

That didn't mean going from park pick-ups to actual friend-friends with Nona hadn't been without its own tricksyness. Even when you find a keeper, you still have to make her one, and it's a giant leap from the kind of friendship that won't withstand a change of kindy day to fully fledged palhood that survives everything — rotavirus, biting, nits, jealousy *and* all the children's problems too (ha!). Nona was such good people that I had to be intentional and — game-changer — honest, about it. Since telling the lies mothers tell had got me more Denifers than Girl-Shabs so far, I decided that with Nona I would be daringly truthful.

'It's so boring over here now when you're not around,' I said a couple of weeks after we'd first spoken, in a tone that was studiously casual and not at all how a stalker would speak. 'Sometimes I just stare at your front door and mentally will you to come out for a chat.'

'Just come and get me next time, you dork,' Nona said, not freaked out at all. ''Snot like I'll be busy.'

I hadn't thought of that. It went against everything I'd taught myself about not looking desperate and needy in front of other women. It also made sense — oh my goodness, just go and get her! I could do that. Not every day — *please*, I still had the tiniest bit of self-respect — but every now and again, like I imagine women did in the 1950s, when everybody wasn't so deathly concerned with boundaries or were just as high as kites on Valium and hot for a yack.

After a few weeks of laughing so hardly that we left the park sore, we met at the swings late one afternoon, and just as we settled in, a misty rain started falling. By then, days that didn't begin with a pre–7 a.m. day-planning textual interchange were the exception rather than the rule. We'd been on a million outings and I'd been to her house, but never she to mine. It was the final frontier. As we stared up at the clouds, I plucked up all my courage, knowing what I did about her beautiful interiors and excellent taste, and I asked if she and Bunny wanted to trip up the steps to maison Mason to play. It was nearly baby dinner time anyway, and I had a freezer full of carrot ice cubes ripe for defrosting. No matter how cool you are and how many blousons you own, a night off the bamix is still a treat, is what I told myself.

'Sure! That would be swell,' Nona said. 'If I make another tuna and white sauce this week, I'll barf.' She ran into her house and came out with a bottle of champagne. We crossed the road all together, a lot of team hand holding and dolly dragging, and I tried to think of a way of getting in ahead of her to turn the sofa cushions to the less stainy side. Couldn't be done. This was going to be raw. My wrists were itchy with nervousness and the possibility that her seeing inside the apartment would somehow change things. It is always awkward that first time a friendship moves from neutral territory into the very heart of private space. You can attempt it too early, and seeing someone's wet bath mat before time can overwhelm a friendship before it has a chance to take.

Not long ago, Minky was invited to her first sleepover. At 9.45 p.m., the father rang and asked us to come get her. 'She's pretty upset; not really sure what happened,' he said, embarrassed. Letting her go was a mistake, I decided instantly. She'd obviously been witness to a foul domestic argument or been made to watch some older brother's grotesque YouTubery.

'It's OK, Minky, you can tell me, what happened?' I asked after I retrieved her. We were lying in my bed, me rubbing her back, her still sobbing.

'It's just,' Minky said after 20 minutes, 'it's just that' — heave — 'they sometimes' — sniff — 'the mum told me, they sometimes have McDonald's. And that's just *not of our family.*'

I was worried that Nona seeing something in my house that was not of her family would make her run for it. But we got inside, and she looked around and said, 'Well, this is just as lovely as toast,' then prised open the champagne with a fork. 'What's our favourite noise, Bun?'

Bunny threw her arms up in the air and shouted 'DOP,' an excellent imitation of the sound a champagne cork makes, especially for an infant. 'Fancy a champoo?' She poured me a glass and raised hers. 'To not having a job! Woo woo.' I raised mine and we clinked, hungry as we were, for drinking.

On high rotation in my kitchen CD player at the time was Joni Mitchell's *Blue*. Shab cannot do more than two Joni Mitchell songs in a row before he starts to make involuntary falsetto wailing sounds, so I have to get all the femmy folk moaning out of my system during working hours. One of the songs — 'Carey', I think — says something about a Mermaid Café, where freaks and soldiers and tourists meet to drink.

'Hey, we are the Mermaid Café!' said Minky, so pleased with herself.

'We're certainly not short on freaks,' Nona said, upending her glass.

We were open for business, then, the Mermaid Café, at least three nights out of five, hers or mine, for the next two years. Eventually the frozen carrot was replaced by real dinners. The bamix switched to a fork, then later we ditched the fork. The babies got bigger and bigger, and only the champoo and Pine O Cleen Wipes remained a constant. Then, one day, our lease ran out and we had to move. The only sorrow in leaving that apartment was not being neighbours with Nona any more. I was worried that our friendship wouldn't survive once driving, not just road crossing, was involved. Ooh, hang on, my phone just pipped.

'Fancy a merm? We're outside with so much dong-dongs.'

I should go and open the front door.

13

NOCTURNE IN B

BY EARLY 2008, BITSY HAD BEEN AWAKE FOR ROUGHLY TWO
years. She had been crying for two-thirds of that time,
irrespective of whether it was dark or light, she was hungry
or fed, wet, dry, sick, well, happy, angry or just killing time.
She had never, before her second birthday, slept for more than
three hours in a row. Since we lived by then in a sort of open-
plan house with only one internal door that boasted the same
sound-dampening qualities as a rice cake, nobody was getting
any sleep. She would go to bed OK but by 9.30 p.m., just as
Shab and I were deciding whether to crack into another disk
of 'The West Wing' or go to bed, she would start to cry. We
would go in, she would cry louder. We would stay out; she
would start to scream. Shab would sneak in and rescue Minky,

who shared the same bedroom, before she was woken up by Bitsy — who would be by then standing up and shouting and flicking the light on and off even though I had stuck a Band-Aid over it to prevent her from doing that. She would start trying to claw her way out of the cot, and pressing her back in was like trying to stuff an angry cat into a supermarket eco tote and knot the handles while it writhed and scratched. It was horrible and heartbreaking and it went on for hours and hours every night, we didn't know why. And before you ask, did we try ... yes, we did. And that, and that, and the other thing twice. The following morning, she would get out of bed happy, but as the day wore on and she grew tired, she would start to lose control. Her oncoming tantrum felt like a freight train on the horizon, viewed from a prone position on the tracks. Tied down, sock in mouth, nothing you could do but wait to get run over.

The cause, it turned out, was just Bitsy. I didn't know it then; I was still hoping her desperate sleeping habits were diet related or something we could sleep-train away. Eventually we worked out that the root of the problem was just Bitsy's extra-special (sarcasm alert!) temperament. While Minky never necessitated a single child-safe latch and had only two moods — happy and concerned, both of which were easily mitigated — Bitsy was born wily, unafraid and eager to displease. Minky fervently believed until she was five that the man up the front of church doing all the talking must actually *be* Jesus and treated him with accordant reverence ('Mum, *look*, Jesus is packing away the microphones'), while Bitsy, age two, told the same man that she was 'sick of your talkin' sounds', adding with a sigh, 'You need talkin' lessons.' Whereas simply threatening to use a big voice on Minky, not actually using one, has her running back into my arms for a dose of reassurance and approval, if Bitsy senses that she's already in trouble, her special Bitsy logic dictates that it's time to take out the trash and really get some bad stuff done. If there's a consequence coming anyway, why not make it a cover-all job? At the first birthday party the nerds were ever invited to, a horrified Minky spat a Twistie into my hand and said, 'Oh Mum, these carrots is *weird*,' while Bitsy sat at the table the entire time pressing Cheezels and jelly and Tiny Teddies into her mouth with a flat hand, while letting others stand in her peripheral vision and chat.

I've often sat and watched Bitsy at home, as she tips juice into a double adaptor or chases a terrified Minky around the house with my GHDs right after they've been switched off and are still 245 degrees, shouting 'Hot crocodile, hot crocodile', and thought that it's lucky she's pretty. Otherwise she'd be a truly loathsome individual. Despite my constant efforts to deplete her vast storehouse of self-esteem, Bitsy remains thoroughly convinced of her own excellence. When we walk into a public place, she will scan the area for a target, walk up to the chosen person and stand in front of them, bashfully toeing the ground, until she gets a compliment. Invariably it comes. 'Aren't you sweet?', 'Oh, don't you have lovely blonde hair?', 'What beautiful skin!' the unwitting object will say, not realising they've been manipulated by a preschooler as naturally sweet as Shirley Temple supping on a Mountain Dew. While it may be true that she has nice curls and throws a great tan eight months of the year, it's hard to really rejoice in those attributes when the child who possesses them has just spent the hour of her intended day-sleep silently painting a mural above her cot with nappy cream. Not just once, a bunch of times, even though I'd started storing the Sudocrem on high shelves, under loose floorboards or putting the whole jar inside a condom and swallowing it, so she couldn't find it. 'Aw dorry, Mummy, I made a bad choice,' she'd say with an utterly unrepentant look on her face, as I walked in to behold a new emollient wallscape. 'I did 'nother cweam painting.'

Everything to do with Bitsy and that cot was chafing, though, so I suppose she was just translating what we all felt about night-time into art. After 18 months of her nocturnal psychosis, I started to dread the onset of evening. I wished it would just stay light all the time. If only we could all stay up on Red Bull and Panadeine Forte and never listen to another spine-melting scream from behind the bedroom door. I had to have some surgery when Bitsy was nearly two and I was so excited about an overnight in hospital and especially the anaesthetic, I told Nona one day. 'I think,' she said, 'that if you're looking forward to a *general* as some "me toime"' — she hit single-finger air quotes — 'there is something wrong.'

The first time Bitsy ever slept through the night, instead of spending the most part of it making fake vomming noises and gnawing on the bars of her cot so that she came to breakfast with white paint flakes around her mouth, was the night she spent with a dozen electrodes glued to her forehead in a $1,500-a-night paediatric sleep clinic. Out like a light from seven till seven was our Bits. When the specialist fast-forwarded through her closed-circuit sleep video and analysed the print outs from her brain scan, he smiled weakly and said: 'You've been had. Cheque or savings?' I really had my fingers crossed for apnoea or, at the very least, a restricted windpipe. Baseless rage and a ferocious personality are harder problems to solve, and we would just have to wait it out.

There are many consequences to extreme sleep deficit, but for me, it manifested itself in the following ways:

- Talking too fast and too much to strangers, especially other mothers.
- Breakfasting daily on double-shot lattes and pharmacy-only headache tablets.
- A hair-trigger temper and regular bouts of weeping.
- Not being able to sleep when I actually had the chance, because I was too scared that I would be

woken up five minutes later. Apparently that's a real thing, postnatal insomnia, but I don't know if you can claim to have it when your baby is walking. I think that's like calling your fatness 'baby weight' when your youngest has a driver's licence.

- Feeling too numb with fatigue to carefully navigate the car out of any underground car park. Most times, I'd just smash my way out of the Woolworths parking lot and feel no remorse.

On two or three very bad nights I dragged my pillows and duvet out to the garage and got a couple of hours' shuteye in the car. They were dark days, but despite the tiredness and the private resentment towards the child who was becoming widely known as 'typical Bitsy', as she neared one, I decided I would throw a birthday party for her. I didn't feel like I had the energy for celebrating, but that is the blessedly amazing thing about maternal love, it makes you do a whole world of things you don't have the energy for. Besides, for all the screaming and scratching and crying, I still had a dynamic, lovable little nerd who deserved to celebrate her first year of living. I called in a Special Occasion Rally, a Festive Rally, sister to the Christmas Rally, which, children or no, you'll be familiar with.

It was quite something, especially since as well as being tired to the point of car accidents, I also hate birthdays generally. All

birthdays, I hate them — mine, the children's, yours, anybody's.
I don't care about getting older or anything. In fact, when
you're frequently mistaken for a teen mother, getting older is
a birthday's only upside. It's that I hate how birthdays become
a mandatory stock-take day: who remembered, who loves you,
how much do they love you, who loves you this year compared
to last, and, of course, in my case, do I have a house yet? No.
Hey, happy birthday! When there are children, though, with
their boundless excitement and yet-unbroken hearts, it is a
mother's job to pretend at least that she's beyond psyched. You
can't lie in bed all day watching text messages not arrive. You
have to make a party and make it last from the 6 a.m. wake-up
to the 6.45 p.m. sugar low. I decided to invite Nona and Bunny,
Girl-Shab and her two children, two other mothers and their
toddlers from playgroot, and Snooch.

Bitsy's birthday is in July, which in Sydney means it's
technically winter but only until 10 a.m., when it's summer again
until at least 3 p.m. I decided we would have it in the Botanical
Gardens, because you cannot party well with toddlers in a two-
bedroom apartment, upstairs. I sent out invitations made of
card and shaped like red and green apples, cut by me, glued by
Minky, torn up by Bitsy, redone by me later that night. The day
before the party I made a carrot cake, an organic one with so
much pricey dried fruit inside and mascarpone icing on top I
could have bought a dozen Michel's Patisserie Barbie cakes for

the same money. I filled party bags; I ironed Bitsy's dress, which had apple-shaped pockets, and put out her apple-red shoes. For those 24 hours, I rallied with such creativity and enthusiasm, you could have launched a lifestyle blog off the back of it.

The day began like other days, at 3 a.m. with Bitsy freaking out in her bed for two hours, then at 5 a.m., Shab took her for an early-morning drive to the beach so Minky and I could get another hour. I had forgotten until just now that he had done that nearly every morning since Bitsy was eight weeks old. I should add that back onto the marital ledger because all this time I've been keeping score without that particular act of heroism factored in. When they returned around 7 a.m., Shab with two coffees and two bloodshot eyes, we sat in bed and opened presents and took photos, while outside it began to rain.

I wondered whether to 'call it off' or 'forge ahead and hope for the best' — every mother of a birthday child has wrestled this precise version of risk and uncertainty. I kept hoping it would clear, while realising that, like beach weddings, park birthdays are always better in the planning stages. Especially in July. I got dressed and tidied up, looking out the window on a three-minutely basis and willing the pockets of blue sky to spread. They didn't. I texted around: 'Come to us at 10am instead. Too wet for park.' Nona arrived early and first, wearing a flopsy floral blouson, navy and hot pink, cinched in at the waist, and a smear of fluorescent pink lipstick. 'It looked so pretty in the rain but now it's sunny out I feel like a hooker,' she said as we both looked out the back door to see that it was now, at T minus five minutes, totally blue out. We decided to forge ahead inside and hope for the best.

The last guest arrived and propped her just-standing infant son against the sofa while she ran to the bathroom. Bitsy pulled herself up next to the child, and with one, I cannot say for sure, *accidental* thrust of her arm, pushed him backwards into the hard marble tile around the fireplace. The child broke his fall with his head. If you had seen blood gushing out of a baby's head with such force and direction in a movie, you would have taken marks off the special-effects department for overdoing it. It was torrential. The child wailed. Minky ran to her room and slammed the door, overwhelmed by the drama. I picked him up and felt blood running over my hand. Bitsy looked small and bereft standing alone by the fireplace. The mother emerged from the bathroom, summoned out by all the screaming: 'Oh, oh, oh, oh, ooooooh!' she cried, cantering towards her son.

'I think he hit his head,' I said weakly. 'I mean, he did hit his head. Bitsy pushed him over.'

'Ugh, typical Bitsy!' the mother said, exasperated.

Again with the blood. I burst into tears. I heard Minky crying in her bedroom. Bitsy started screaming because nobody was holding her. I was mad at her but, because she was mine, I also felt desperately sorry for her. I wanted to defend her. It was too sad to think that a child can earn a reputation for awfulness by their first birthday, when just as often she was funny and sweet and amusing. The mother took her boy and held a soon-soaked flannel to the back of his head. Nona and the other guests stood awkwardly around the edge of the room wondering if they should forge ahead and hope for the best or make a freaking run for it. It was 10.05 a.m.

I called an ambulance. The blood wasn't stopping. The child gradually stopped crying and Nona manfully brought out the cake, while I sat curled up on the sofa and drank champagne from a mug because Nona couldn't find glasses, which is not like her at all. The child sat next to me on his mother's lap and we let out the same periodic whimpers. The cake was quite nice.

The paramedics arrived. 'Are you the mother?' they asked me, I suppose because I was the only adult crying. I shook my head and led them to the bedroom, where they conducted a thorough examination on a bath towel laid out on my bed. He would be fine, they said. Some ice, some of that special head glue, a little Vanish carpet cleaner and you wouldn't know there'd even been a party.

I would know. Apart from a moment of sweet comic relief when I walked into the kitchen with dirty plates to find another little guest lying on his belly on the table licking the icing off the leftover cake like a very small wildebeest at a watering hole, it was, oh, I'd say, maybe the worst party ever. I had rallied because I really had wanted to celebrate Bitsy with the clutch of lovely friends I had made. I wanted to drink champagne out of a glass and take photos and toast to getting through, but instead, by 11 a.m., the house was empty and I was on my knees scrubbing a now-brown circle of blood out of the carpet. Generally speaking, self-pity is a dangerous place to paddle for a mother, but I dove in headfirst. If we'd had a proper house, or a garden or a sunny day or no stupid fireplace that didn't even work, none of this would have happened, I cried to myself and then to Shab, who called at lunch time to see how it went.

The only solution, I decided as I dragged rubbish out to the bins later that night, was work. Since I was clearly not excelling at motherhood — couldn't throw a party, couldn't teach a baby to sleep — I would throw myself into freelancing and be excellent at that instead. I had kept writing from home ever since Spackers handed me a ready-made career just after Minky was born. When we moved back to Australia, I kept writing features to ship back to *The Times*, and then, as I built new contacts at home, I wrote for magazines — lifestyle, fashion and womensy sorts of titles. I liked it, and the money was very helpful, but after the birth of Our Lady of the Perpetual Wakefulness, I had let my output dwindle to a feature a month. Now, I decided, I would write all the time, during every nap and every evening, and on weekends. I would work until I felt in control of something again.

Yeah, it doesn't really work like that. Not after children, I would learn, because the children were about to teach me. The following Monday morning, Shab left for work, and I had to get both girls ready for an 8.45 a.m. occasional-care drop-off so I could write a story. It was something like 'Ten Ways to Please Your Man' for a magazine that publishes stories like that and has a sealed section. The subject was going to be difficult because apart from 'No 1. sexing', which was obvious, I could think of only two more (No 2. not crying, No 3. hot fruit pies) and I didn't think they would pass the editor.

In preparation for the day's work, I had everything perfectly organised — the breakfast dishes put away, beds made, bags packed, children dressed, hatted, shoed and sun-creamed. I was caffeinated and Nurofened and had even managed to tidy my desk and get all my papers and transcripts ready so I could come back from drop-off and sit straight down to it, maximising every costly minute of child-free time. I left the room where the girls were playing to apply a thick coat of concealer to the bruise-dark circles under my eyes, and when I came back a minute later, Bitsy and Minky had decided to climb up onto my desk and do a little light crafting, your basic glitter-and-clag affair.

I have a love/hate relationship with glitter. On one hand, I appreciate its alluring sparkliness and the extra pop it brings to an otherwise meat-and-potatoes pasting project. At the same time, I resent how it sticks to your face, multiplies upon opening and always, always, gets knocked over by a three-year-old's bumbling elbow or tipped out on purpose by a remorseless one-year-old. Shab once spent ten minutes in the work bathrooms trying to remove a lone square of glitter from beneath his eye, which had arrived there via an art project, the floor, my hand and my hair, finally settling on his face during a session of No. 1–style man-pleasing the evening after that crafternoon.

An entire canister of multicoloured glitter had been upended all over my desk, my computer, all my material, the carpet and the glue-covered children themselves. 'Bitsy all farkly!' she announced as I walked, horrified, mouth agape, towards the farkling crime scene. Minky's favourite, most precious baby doll was lying on the floor, also covered in tiny pieces of rainbow. I picked it up by the leg and flung it at the wall, like the Trunchbull doing hammer toss. I *aimed* for the wall, but actually the hard-headed plastic baby bounced off the wall and hit the lower pane of a sash window, which exploded on impact, showering the room with hundreds of sharp, thick shards. The three of us burst into tears. I called Shab, who wasn't even off the bus yet, and asked him to come home, setting a new personal best for a not-coping call-back. It wasn't even 9 a.m. He walked in 20 minutes later, to find two terrified, glitter-covered children rocking back and forth, trying to soothe each other on Minky's bed, his wife sitting numb and silent at the kitchen table, and a broken window.

'Wow, OK,' he said, as he crunched across the living room carpet. 'New low.'

'Please don't ask,' I said thinly.

He calmed the children, taped some paper over the window, hoovered up the glass fragments, made me a pot of green tea and took the children to occasional care before returning to work, a little farkly himself. I got my story done (No 4. not breaking windows, No. 5 general keeping it together) and apologised over and over to both girls when I picked them up.

'No throwing!' I sometimes say now when they're lobbing apple-sized rocks at each other in the park.

'But Mummy throws things,' Bitsy will reply. ''Member when you threw baby Poppy at the window and you broked it,' she adds in case I don't.

'Poppy's a toy,' I then say to any adult in earshot, with a hard, nothing-to-see-here smile.

I feel bad about it still. Breaking a window with one of your daughter's best-loved toys in front of her is to be avoided where possible. I was just so tired. I was so, *so* tired, and exhaustion makes you do less-than-excellent things. A woman I knew from London had three children in three years and was living the same trifecta of time-poor/cash-poor/poor-poor as us. Her outlet during those first awful years, she told me later, was slamming the pantry door repeatedly and so hard that plates and jars inside it broke. Her husband knew not to ask why they were getting so short on crockery, and still, in her house, a too-hard day is referred to as 'a real three plater'. Another friend found that driving laps around the city playing 50 Cent's 'That Ain't Gangsta' as loud as the car stereo will go and shouting 'Mummy can't hear you, Mummy can't hear you' at her anxious children in the back was an effective means of self-soothing in the preschool years.

Knowing that other women have destroyed household property out of anger makes me feel better about the Poppy-tossing episode. What made me feel worse was the fact that for an entire year after that — 12 calendar months — we didn't have enough spare cash to get the window fixed, so every day, as a gentle breeze whistled through the apartment, I was reminded just how much rallying plus more work plus a lot of wishing were not adding up to a better version of our life. I felt worn down from three years of semi-solo, sleep-deprived, underfunded family life that seemed to lurch from one crisis to the next. Everything was broken and I couldn't fix it, no matter how hard I tried. In a little while longer, it would all fix itself. And after that, we could take care of the window.

14

PIONEER BALL

IT TURNS OUT YOUR HUSBAND WILL NEVER LOOK HOTTER THAN when he's playing Pioneer Ball, a funny kind of Slavic volleyball, with an orphan. I have seen it with my own two peepers and, surely, it's a lust-inducing vista.

Somebody said, 'Never make big decisions when you're tired', or maybe it was, 'Don't shop angry' and I misheard, but post-Bitsy there was no time I wasn't tired, and decisions still had to be made. It was too hard, everything: our life, the house, the bebes, the No Fruit Mondays, the psychotic exhaustion that translated into thousands of dollars worth of smash repair. I had broken a window and been offered more SSRIs than other mothers have polished off 5 p.m. baby-dinner scraps, and I didn't have another rally in me. Something had to change, but we'd tried almost everything I could think of already. We'd moved countries, and, although it had helped for a while, it hadn't solved anything long term, only replacing special London problems with Sydney ones. Moving house again would take more out than it put in, although a few more opening and closing doors might have been nice. We were careful, but we never had money. I longed and longed and longed for a real home but we were no closer to getting one. All the number crunching and placing calls to long-day-care centres still couldn't make my going back to work full time financially advantageous. We were both pedalling furiously but making not one inch of ground. Something *had* to change.

Minky scars easily, and one day when she was about four, I found her standing in front of the mirror examining a mosquito bite on her face, which she had scratched and turned into a deep purple mound. We both knew that wasn't going away any time soon, and she was miserable about it. 'Every time I get another scar,' she said dolefully, 'my face just gets a bit more ruined.' That's how I felt about our life. Every time something — a coming home from hospital, a birthday party, the lost job — fell short of my stupid dumb expectations about how life should look, everything just got a bit more ruined.

Soon after the fun-times realisation that our life fundamentally wasn't working, I met a woman called Elsa who had just moved back from Russia with her husband and a son the same age as

Bitsy. They had been working in orphanages during term time, then staffing the state-run summer camps where all the orphans go for a bit of fresh air in the holidays. Don't start making sicking noises. I'm not going to get worthy or use the phrase 'make a difference' non-sarcastically. You know I'd never use up brain space on third world issues when I could be thinking about myself. I am expert, actually, at avoiding eye contact with anyone proffering a bucket or holding a clipboard. I have never bought a raffle ticket in my life, allowed my awareness to be raised in any way, or treated charity clothing bins as anything other than feel-good rubbish bins for regrettable fashion choices.

But something about the photographs Elsa showed me, gosh. They were of a clutch of children the same age as mine, who she said owned one outfit each and nothing else, playing in an empty concrete swimming pool painted in a sickly Slavic green and shot through with weeds. They had large, sunken eyes and rosy cheeks against pale skin, which reminded me of Bitsy's permanently exhausted facial pallor. You never want orphans to remind you of your own children, because suddenly they're not just pictures in a beseeching brochure any more, they're real little tinies with no parents, no-one to adore them and write down the funny things they say and clean up when they tip dinner off the plate because it tastes 'like football', as Bitsy did at least twice a week. There is no-one for them to climb into bed with when there is a scary noise outside or just because they feel like it.

I couldn't get the Russian children out of my mind. I told Shab about them, and, although he is generally more compassionate and caring than me, he would most likely have forgotten about them soon enough, in the way you do when the original revelation wasn't yours. I kept talking about them, and thinking about them as I pushed the nerds on the swings or lay awake at night being kicked in the abdomen by Minky's hard little heels. I looked at flights. I googled 'Russia + communicable diseases + children'. I made some calls to the agency that sent Elsa and her family there. You could go for as little as three weeks, they said. You could make a difference in a short time, they said, and for once I didn't roll my eyes. It will change your life too, they said. Promise?

Shab said he would run the numbers. He did. It would clean us out, he said. All the money we had, the already diminished nest egg we'd brought back from London and been pretending was still going to buy us a house one day, would be gone. Somehow that made me want to do it more. Like a Bitsy in trouble, my reasoning went: we are already mildly screwed, so why not get in deeper? Let's forget about houses, future private school applications, Sydney's crazy-making, glossy values and go do something. Reset our priorities, get over ourselves. Let's stop trying so hard and *really* mess things up. It would also be good, I thought, to teach the nerds a little compassion. Although we weren't wealthy, they were still privileged and right on track, developmentally, to become self-obsessed white girls with no sense of the world beyond the café on our corner. At the time, Minky was on a Dolly Parton jag, listening to a lot of 'Jolene' and 'Nine to Five' and 'My Tennessee Mountain Home', which includes a line about Dolly growing up with holes in her shoes.

'Dolly Partnin must have been wearing Crocs, Mum,' Minky said thoughtfully. There could be no other explanation.

Six weeks later, we were on a flight to Finland, our veins coursing with every travel inoculation money could buy. No tetanus, yellow fever, typhoid or heps A, B and C for Team Mason. Bitsy cried for 20 of the 24 hours it took to reach Helsinki, rejecting our every attempt to console her. Food, pacifiers, treats, walking, sitting, lying down, sweets, being up, being down, television, singing — nothing worked. She cried furiously, writhing around in our arms, her face sweaty and crimson. Shab, who never loses his shiz, started to lose his shiz.

'Could you breast-feed her?' he asked.

'I weaned her eleven months ago,' I replied.

'I know. But if you really, really wanted to, could you like ...'

What? As if! Was he *crackers*? If he was, I couldn't tell, having lost my shiz at least 12 hours before.

'I'll go to the bathrooms and check.'

I could not, although I gave my breasts such a thorough fondling in there, it was like a mile-high club for one.

After a night repacking and stocking up on extra meds, bulk craft supplies, insect repellent and snack food in Helsinki (and also, truth be told, making a frenzied smash-and-grab through the H&M children's wear department) we took a four-hour train ride to a town called Vyborg, which is one of the first Russian towns over the border. You know the exact moment when you cross over from Finland to Russia, because everything suddenly gets a bit more ruined. The little houses beside the train tracks looked like they were held together with spit and earth. There were abandoned factories and long-deserted building sites every few miles; and the people, who would just stand and watch the train as it passed, with heavy loads on their backs, looked broken. It was beautiful and eerie, with the strangest light and oddest soul of any place I've been. Vyborg itself was like North End Road on steroids. Russians would put a Club Med on North End Road if they had means. 'All chicken you can eat!' they'd say. 'Beautiful pigeon!' 'Lovely plastic washing basket, choice of colours only £1!'

We were picked up from Vyborg's town square by a Camp Kastyor staffer in a blue transit van that lacked seat belts, suspension or padding of any kind on its backwards-facing bench seats. Minky and Bitsy were already smashed from the five days of travel that had got us this far, so they lay on our laps with their fingers jammed in their ears. When we arrived at the camp two hours later, the last 45 minutes of which had been spent revving and grinding up a dirt road, it was 4 p.m. and as hot and bright as noon. I forgot that high summer in the far Northern Hemisphere would mean nearly a month without darkness. A sun that never sets was like a dream come true for Bitsy, so that was an early win for her. Since the children were all resting in their dorms when we fell out of the van, we wandered around the camp site. Minky needed to go to the bathroom. There wasn't one. The 200 children and their leaders used pit toilets in little huts set back from the camp's concreted central square, in patches of straggly birch forest. OK! Average to below-average start for me, I thought, gazing through the semi-darkness of the stall into a flyblown long drop, which truth be told, could have been longer. Minky and I backed out, our noses and mouths buried in our sleeves, and found a tree for her a bit further afield.

At 4.30 p.m., Ricky Martin's 'Livin' La Vida Loca' played over the Tannoy, and the children started straggling out of their rooms, swinging bags of hard lollies and half-eaten buns. I was already feeling a little keyed up, O, H and S wise; what I had seen of Camp Kastyor so far didn't make it a standard-bearer in the child-safety department, what with those rusty drums of dark-brown rainwater sunk into the ground, sawn-off drainpipes jutting out of various walls at five-year-old eyeball height, and row upon row of iron beds with edges like guillotines. Once the children came out and, as a gesture of friendship, started biting off pieces of their buns and poking them straight into Bitsy's mouth, so that entire, grubby fingers vanished into her little open beak, I realised I was going to have to recalibrate my maternal hazard meter for these few weeks.

We hadn't really explained to Bitsy and Minky the concept of orphanhood, and since some of the children at the camp weren't orphans, just sponsored by the state and sent there from disadvantaged homes, it wasn't technically lying to brush over the whole parent-free state of things. It wouldn't have mattered if we'd given the nerds a point-by-point briefing on our humanitarian mission, anyway. As soon as they were being piggybacked around the camp with mouths so full of sweets that a ribbon of bright pink drool spooled out of the uncloseable centres, you could tell that as far as they were concerned, this was the best holiday ever. Add in the 11 p.m. bedtime, the fact all four of us were sharing a bunk room, and the near-total absence of ablutionary facilities, except for one shared shower block that had hot water between 10 p.m. and 10.30 p.m. each night, and the nerds were in heaven.

They didn't even mind the food. We filed into the dining hall that first day, at 7 p.m., after another stanza of 'Livin' La Vida Loca' signalled the start of dinner. That song was used instead of a bell for every transition in the day, five or six times a day, and in another three weeks it really had begun to feel like a bullet through my brain, as Mr Martin himself would put it. The food was already on the tables on little floral dinner plates. It definitely looked like animal flesh of some description, pale brown and spongy like a fridge-spoiled mushroom, but after that, your guess as to its origin is as good as mine. There was also buckwheat cooked like rice, soup and bread. The bread became our mainstay. It was nearly black and thickly sliced, and we learned quickly to always finish the entire basketful at each meal, because if you didn't, it just stayed there and curled up at the corners until you did. The kitchen staff didn't refresh the basket until it was empty, so if you left the bread today, you would see it again the next day and the next day, and the following summer. The girls tried everything that was put in front of them, and Minky said the bread was 'just like from Macro', our local organic provedore that sometimes sold us $9 sourdough batards. Dinner was almost the same every night, although the spongy brown meat would be switched out occasionally for canned fish or a sausage the same colour and texture as one of those expensive hairless cats. The camp children all devoured it and then filled their pockets with hard rusks that the cooks made out of crusts left on the children's plates, cut up and fried. I also discovered when I went backstage to the kitchen one day that if you didn't finish your soup, the cooks tipped it back into a central cauldron for the next day.

Our days developed a rhythm quickly. We woke up at 6 a.m., when the sun came upper — when it never goes down you just guess when it is daylight and not nightlight any more. Shab and I took turns running to the pits, which were definitely more bearable before the hot daytime sun turned each stall into a kind of faecal slow cooker. After Minky's first visit to the stalls, she refused to go back. I guess I could have told her to toughen up, but relative to her size, getting one foot on either side of the pit would have been like an adult trying to straddle a hole the size of hula hoop, so I let her skip it. We found a pink plastic potty for her instead at the only shop nearby, which existed, as far as I could tell, to keep the camp security guards in unfiltered cigarettes and the Russian equivalent of *FHM*. I've never envied a child their potty before, but Russia was a time for new experiences. At 7.30 a.m., a few stanzas from our good friend Ricky meant it was breakfast time in the dining room, buckwheat porridge with a swirl of butter in the middle, and a cup of sugar with a small amount of tea in it. It was my favourite meal of the day, so carby, so meatless. Afterwards we wandered outside and played with the children until lunch.

Some were as young as four, the oldest nearly 16 and rocking a pretty awesome angry Russian teen vibe, with a tonne of electric-blue eyeliner and T-shirts with punky-looking slogans printed on them in English, which said completely inoffensive things like 'America Bike' or 'Feel Yourself Russian'. I guess you could read that offensively, but the older children were secretly sweet and ever so proud of their whispering, eye-rolling adolescentness. When we gave out balloons or bubble mixture or press-on tattoos, they held out for about 16 seconds before joining the queue. I say 'queue' but it was more like a flock of urban seagulls going for spilt chips. Before meeting any in real life, I had always imagined orphans as placid and resigned to life's cruelty, maybe a little bit spunky like Annie, but mostly pretty laid-back and grateful. Actually, orphans can be weird and mean. They have to learn to get theirs, since no-one is there to get it for them. Giving things out caused a vicious frenzy and we soon learned not to do it. It was a no as well to competitions with prizes, because who wants to be the person who makes 24 orphans cry by giving a prize to just one? It was better to play games or have cartwheel contests (no prizes, only clapping). Shab played hour after hour of handball — he still had game from Mosman Primary, class of '86 — and the Russian boys thought he was pretty much Jesus, running. I sat for hours in the square painting hundreds of fingernails with glittery polish. We joined the children on occasional field trips to the very lakes I'd all that time ago associated with K'Hunt's rusty jus. The swimming holes were opaque and almost orange, with a strange sulphuric smell, but the children started tearing off their clothes before the camp bus even stopped. Most of them swam in their white underwear, which, because they were thin and often had close-cropped hair, made the entire tableau look pretty Chernobylly, like a *National Geographic* spread from the late 1980s. I couldn't swim in that water, personally, for fear that my skin would surely bubble off, and I worried for all the children who were drinking in great mouthfuls of what looked like undiluted runoff from a nearby smelter. Bitsy and Minky weren't keen either, so there may be an entire tranche of Russian children who understand Australians to be a particularly non-aquatic people. I did join in their discos, learn their dances, compete in their mini-Olympics, share their snacks, and run ad hoc seminars on hygiene, nutrition and dental health, no Russian child's strong suit as far as I could see. A lot of the children had soft, brown stumps where teeth should have been, but since the kitchen staff considered off-brand candy an excellent snack between meals, every meal, it wasn't hard to see why.

Some of the children seemed completely fine, mentally and physically, and maybe just a little bit more eager for attention and lap time with Shab or me than a regular kid. Other children were beyond repair. One girl, Olga, who was overweight, right on the cusp of puberty in that awful mixed-up, greasy way, was scarily flirtatious with Shab. She meowed instead of talking. It was confronting at the start of the camp and no less so by the end. Another girl, Kira, who was known for stealing and had awful sores on her legs, was teased and excluded constantly by the other children, but bless that funny little Bitsy, who decided Kira was her favourite out of everyone. Since time pushing Bitsy in her stroller, doing her hair or feeding her pre-masticated bread was of high value amongst campers, Bitsy's obvious preference for Kira gave that little girl some much-needed cache.

She's nothing if not surprising, that Bitsy, who had her second birthday at Camp Kastyor. She was sung to and given balloons by the camp director, as well as a hoard of second-hand merch — used lip balms, paperclips, that sort of thing — by all her camp fans. She loved every minute of it, when I had felt sure she would spend the entire time protesting the lack of television or fresh food or the fact she was sharing her parents and sister with 200 needy children. The most surprising thing about Bitsy and camp: she chose that place, with its Gulag-grade mattresses, itchy woollen blankets and curtainless dormitories, as the setting for her best-ever sleep. She was out colder than a brain trauma victim every night for 12 straight hours. She napped for two hours in the middle of the day like the camp children and woke up as happy as a pre-Stalin kulak. She lost the dark circles under her eyes, and her previously lacklustre vocabulary began to expand. She'd clearly been too exhausted to learn to talk before, hence all the impotent screaming, but suddenly she was all talkin' sounds without any talkin' lessons. Camp Kastyor gave us, along with diarrhoea and mosquito bites the size of quail eggs, a new improved Bitsy Mason. The cold, infrequent showers in a concrete shower block, the canned fish, the special kind of weariness that comes with looking after your own two children while attempting to connect meaningfully with hundreds of others, was all worth it for Bitsy's own private Russian revolution. By the end, even the pit toilets had ceased to bother me.

OK, that's a lie. They still feature in my dreams. Confession time! We were at camp, after all, and I'm sure the Soviet version of Truth or Dare was happening all around us. Early one morning, about halfway in, I found a way to reduce the frequency of my visits to the pits. At 5 a.m., while my family was sleeping in bunks beside and above me, I climbed out of bed and tiptoed towards the door for that regular morning horsey wee that mothers do. I couldn't face it. It was always freezing early in the morning, and I wanted to climb back into bed for another hour of sleep before Ricky pushed and pulled me down to breakfast. I turned back to face the room and leaned against the door, thinking. There in the corner was Minky's pink potty. Huh. I thought about the flies that would already, despite the hour and the cold, be queuing up for a spot on my face while I used the pit. I walked over to the potty and took it behind one of the bunk beds, as far away from my sleeping husband as I could get. I slid my pyjama bottoms down and crouched over it. As soon as I sat down, I realised I had made a mistake. I shouldn't have done it. What was I going to do with the contents, anyway? I hadn't thought of that and now it was too late. Sensing a seat beneath it, my bladder gave way and suddenly I was, a fully fledged grown-up, doing weewees on the toily. Thirty seconds in, a worse thought came into my mind. The potty was overall quite large but the central receptacle was deceptively shallow, like those cleverly packaged pots of Olay. What if I went over? Surely it must nearly be full by now. Even

Minky could fill this thing after a single juice popper. I closed my eyes and tried to stem the flow, like those Kegel pamphlets I was given in hospital told me to, but my post-bebe pelvic floor wouldn't come to the party. Eventually, it stopped on its own and I stood, cramped of thigh, to survey the tide level. It was half a millimetre from the potty's rounded edge. I stood wondering how to dispose of it. There would surely be some staff about by now who would see me on the five-minute walk to the pits, and even so, getting outside meant pushing open three or four heavy swing doors, and a full potty is not something you can hold with one hand. I would have to tip it out the high window of our dorm, into the deserted forest behind it. It was my only option, although to do so meant walking it past Shab and climbing up onto the shelves we were using as a dining table for the girls' regular pre-dinner dinner of Nutella from Helsinki on rice cakes from Sydney. I walked across the dorm room holding the potty, with the concentrated steadiness of a child carrying a loaded breakfast tray down the hallway on Mother's Day. I placed it on the shelf, climbed up and opened the window. Shab woke up, rolled over and silently watched, bleary-eyed, as his wife tipped a plastic potty full of her own urine out a window.

'Romance never dies,' he said, before rolling back over.

I know, so gross. How could I do such a thing? I don't know, but I did — every morning for the rest of camp. A very special kind of me time, is how I remember it.

We had one scheduled day off in the middle of the camp, and we were driven to the outskirts of St Petersburg, about two hours away, where the subway line started. As we got out, the driver said in Russian something like 'Smell you later' and screeched off, leaving us in front of a giant concrete housing compound. We took the train into the centre of town and spent seven miserable, aimless hours walking around that crowded, crumbling city, an eerie re-imagining of my first too-long outings in London with Minky. Our credit card was sucked into a cash machine on the Nevsky Prospect, the queue for the Hermitage was four hours long and it was scorchingly hot by midday. Bitsy had her stroller but Minky needed to be carried the entire time. I had decided to wear flip-flops, and when I climbed back into the van that night, I noticed that my feet were, as the lyricist R Martin would say, the colour mocha. We did spend a pleasant hour in the children's section of the Dom Knigi bookshop, and we used their regular, normal flushing toilets three times each. I would have eaten caviar and blinis off those toilets, after Camp Kastyor's pits.

The second half of the camp was the same as the first, with some new children coming and other ones going. Everyone, including staffers at the agency, had told us we would be sorry to say goodbye to particular children. I was, especially Kira, because she and Bitsy had become so tight, and another little boy, called Tolek, who looked like a mini version of Shab and was feisty and funny and passionately devoted to all four of us. More than I was to any of the children, though, I was sad to say goodbye to Katya, one of the camp cleaners. She was in her seventies and had hair like cotton wool, and bright blue eyes. She cleaned the dorm-room floors with cold water and newspaper when the spirit moved her, but most of the time she just sat on a bench in her apron, watching the children play. She once told Shab, who was working on a nice camp beard, that he should shave, lest all that stubble stop he and I from having 'passionate times'. That she thought we would be having passion in a Soviet bunk room, going three days between showers and using Pine O Cleen Wipes for our intimate cleansing, says much about the hardiness of the Russian soul. Katya and I had struck up a bit of a friendship ever since we wound up in the shower block at the same time one night. She spoke effusively to me in Russian, totally naked except for brown business socks and black plastic sandals, which she wore in and out of the shower. I pretended to know what she was talking about, although, with the translator we were paying for back in the dorms, I was lost. I nodded, smiled, and tried to stay covered up and get clean at the same time. I liked her so much, our Bonus Babushka.

On our last day, as Shab was hauling our bags out to the blue van, I took the girls to go and say goodbye and give Katya the thank-you cards they had made. She was standing outside her little cabin, which was just big enough for a narrow bed and a

chest of drawers. She took me inside by the hand, opened the
top drawer and gave me a bag of chocolate biscuits for the train
and a small plastic house as a present. It looked like the 'Play
School' house, with a front door painted in the middle and two
windows below a little red roof. I put it in my pocket, and when
she hugged me to her enormous Russian bosom, I cried like
an overstimulated baby. Then, two hours in the van back to
Vyborg; four hours on the train to Helsinki, where we bought
box after box of fresh raspberries and ate salmon and potatoes
by the harbour; and straight to a flight lounge we paid royally
to get into at Helsinki-Vantaa Airport. We rolled through the
doors looking like homeless people and stood under the shower,
all four of us together, for 45 minutes, and sullied maybe two
dozen white towels.

Back home, the house seemed so quiet and still after all the
noise of camp and vans and night flights. In the silence, I could
hear the fridge whirring. I sat thinking, looking out the kitchen
window at our travel clothes drying on the washing line (after
three cycles each they still smelled like liver and buckwheat, so
in my final act of charity I drove them to the nearest Anglicare
bin). There was only a hole now where our savings had been.
Now, also, there was a little plastic house on the windowsill
above my sink and a funny new realisation that had first flittered
into my mind as Shab and I washed the girls' slippery little bodies
in the Helsinki Airport lounge and saw weeks of camp dirt

running off them: I liked us. I liked how we did things. I liked that we didn't have a single cross word with each other during all that travel, that we invented the game Leave or Retrieve to make the toilets bearable. ('If your wedding ring dropped down there, would you leave it or retrieve it?' We eventually settled on only passport and child would we retrieve. Everything else could stay right where it landed.) I loved the time Shab and I spent in our dorm after the girls fell asleep, whispering to each other and eating Nutella off the non-bristly ends of our toothbrushes in the absence of cutlery. I liked watching Shab attempt Russian folk dancing or try to keep a straight face as the teenagers read out their self-penned poetry. (The thematic canon of teen poetry is universal, as it turns out. Even orphans hate their parents.) I misted up watching the girls hug and kiss all their new friends goodbye. And now we were home and we were OK. We had done it all wrong — the wrong country, the wrong time, with no preparation — but for the first time since Minky was born, I started to think Team Mason was going to make it. We had so much less and so much more than we started with. We had made a difference.

15

SO, YOU'RE GOING BACK TO WORK!

THE PERIOD SPENT AT HOME WITH BABIES, HOWEVER LONG, IS like camp: intense, emotional, a lot of time toughing it out around adventure playground equipment. And like camp, it can't last forever. People start leaving. Sure, they'll sign your T-shirt and promise to stay BFFs 4evs, but it doesn't always happen.

The bonds formed between postpartum women are fast and firm, but as the babies head towards their first birthdays, formerly oversubscribed mothers groups start to feel like the last Sunday at Paradise Valley. All the cool people are missing. It's not as much fun as before. Only the die-hards and hangers-on remain, sucking back their mochas and talking about who's gone back where, for how many days a week, with what childcare arrangement. Those who stay behind can feel — passive-aggressively strong language coming — not a little bit betrayed. When Girl-Shab went back to her accounting job four days a week, forcing an end to our four years of Thursday mornings, I felt like somebody had died. We'd had a good run. I could hardly accuse her of being hasty, but I still felt lost for the next six months, on Thursdays particularly, between 10 a.m. and noon. Once she decided to go back, it happened so quickly I never even had a chance to say goodbye or sign her T-shirt. I tried returning to the same playground at the same time, without her, but that made it worse. If Nona ever picks up a few days a week of something, I will feel bereft all over again — only this time, I won't be unprepared. This time, I have a letter waiting in my desk drawer. Some of the details will need filling out, but I'm reproducing it here so that if you are a stay-at-homer betrayed one day in that cruellest of ways, you can use it to bring about much-needed closure.

Dear one-time friend, [insert name here],

So, you have decided to go back to work. That is sad.

We've become quite close these last 15 months, since fate and the [insert suburb] Early Childhood Centre thrust us together. We have spent so much time together, laughing, chatting, comparing our babies' development relentlessly, in private and out loud. We have been to every park between your house and mine countless times, giving each its own had-to-be-there nickname (sandy park, the vomit park, the one with the thing). Lately, we've even started going out on girls' nights and getting totally smashed on a glass each of pinot because our alcohol tolerance is still so low. We've made some real memories, [insert nickname here], and I will miss having you on the circuit.

At the same time, I must confess to feeling a little hurt by your return to the workaday world. It has been unexpected to say the least. So many times, over chais at the horsey park, you said you were going to 'play it by ear' work wise, that you definitely wouldn't be going back full time, and not even part time, until [insert child's name here] was in a big boy's bed, although, to be honest, I thought at the time that that was a strangely arbitrary deadline. Of course, I didn't say anything. We even talked, you'll remember, about launching a funky children's-wear website together, lotsagear4bubs.com.au, which we agreed would be a great way to 'keep our brains ticking over' and 'something we can do from home, in our own time'. I hope you won't be offended if I forge ahead with that plan by myself, although I will change the name since you thought it up. I also plan to sell hampers and those baby-shower cakes made out of nappies, which means it's not the exact model we talked about. I also have an idea for a children's book.

I hope that we will stay friends. Still, I am wondering who, from the few remaining members of mothers group, I might sub on to replace you, since you will no longer be of any use to me during the week. And, truth be told, since [your husband's name] and [her husband's name] don't get on all that well — remember that Saturday morning at [child-friendly beach] when they expressed forcefully divergent opinions on [insert topic] — I don't imagine we'll manage to hook up on the weekends, although we both insisted we would when you broke the news.

If you'll allow me to speak freely, I worry that once you switch sides and become the kind of self-important working mother we always made such sport of, we will realise we have little in common after all. I worry you will use the word 'juggling' too often and without irony, and that you will seek to diminish the hard work and complexity of my typical day in order to justify yours. I fear you will poke holes in the business model behind bubsgear-n-hampers.com.au once you have reconnected with your professional self.

So, in a way, I suppose, this is goodbye and thank you — for all the chai and lifts home from group, for the hours spent together in shopping centres and drizzly parks, and for not minding when [your child's name] bit [her child's name], just as I did not mind when you still came to group right after [her child's name] had had the vomits and we all came down with it over Easter.

I wish you well in your new endeavour, and I hope that [her child's name] is not scarred or her development seriously retarded by your daily absence. Say hello to the outside world for me.

Fondest regards,

[sign here]

x

P.S. Can I get all my *InStyle*s back?

The impetus for Girl-Shab's return to work was the fact that our oldest children were about to be five. Big school was coming. The only upside to her timing: I had fewer hours to kill drinking coffee in playgrounds, because of the hours I was now putting into worrying about school. Not Minky's readiness or whether we'd chosen the right one — I was worried about my first day with School Mothers. Would I have anybody to play with? Who would I sit with during lines? I was in straits. I didn't know anybody with school-age children, and, although there is an abundance of literature to help children prepare, there are no illustrated 'First Experience' books for parents called *So You're Off to Big School: Don't Overdo the Bronzer Because the Other Mothers Will Think You're Cheap!* My tactic, I decided, would be to make a good impression upfront and hope everything would follow from there. I planned a first-day ensemble down to the last button. Had it been able to speak, my outfit would have been all 'What? Hey? Oh hey' — just totally casual and confidently alluring. When the day came, I straightened my hair until I could have snapped it off like taffy and then mussed it right back up again to show how devoted I was to the kind of hands-on mothering that doesn't allow time for personal grooming.

Minky had been dressed and ready — with hat, shoes, ankle-grazing gingham dress and oversize backpack hoisted on her shoulders and clipped at the waist — at 4.50 a.m., and a mere three hours later, it was time to go. Bitsy was two and a half by then, and we had just graduated from her giant, expensive stroller to a cheap, collapsible one from Kmart that I could leave outside our front door between uses and not worry about it being boosted by a passer-by. Looking back, only someone truly desperate would have stolen the Mason family stroller, as crusted as it was in a hard outer layer of reconstituted cracker, but still I used to worry about it. A cheap stroller I cared less about was a relief. As I strapped Bitsy in that first day, I noticed that the foam around the handles had split and started to unfurl. It looked a little tacky. School Mothers might judge me. Although Minky was trying to climb over our front gate by now, in a desperate bid to begin her formal education, I decided to run back inside, root around in the cutlery drawer for a tube of Super Glue and just ever so quickly stick that handle down. It would take two seconds. Back outside, I ran a generous line of glue around the handle and pressed the foam to the metal, holding it there for a second while it dried. As it turns out, the glue people are not kidding around when they suggest not getting their product on your skin. In that tiny moment of pressing, the fleshy part of my palm just below my thumb bonded to the stroller handle.

It was 15 minutes, by then, until Minky's first-ever bell, and I didn't want to be late. Firsts are so often, in the minds of overly analytical mothers, bellwethers for all like days to come. I firmly believed that if Minky was late for her first-ever roll call, it would be a short descent into truancy, exclusion and an HSC that needed to be split over two years. So we set off and, to begin with, the fact I couldn't let go of the stroller mattered little. We walked happily to school, chatting and not holding hands. Minky talked me through her plans for the day and outlined her little hopes and dreams, while I made active-listening noises and, with my spare bit of brain, thought through ways of unsticking my hand without losing my lovely unique palm print. I yanked a little. No movement. Plus it sort of burned. I thought about drenching the area with Minky's drink bottle, but solvency sort of things tend to laugh in the face of water.

I learned that as a teenager, after I tripped carrying a full tub of lava-hot depilatory wax in my parents' en suite the day our house was going to auction and had to scrub it off the textured wallpaper with only tap water and my tears. My hand would have to wait until I had done the drop-off and could slide home past a chemist for a little rubbing alcohol or nail polish remover.

We found Minky's classroom, and she hung up her bag while I leaned nonchalantly on the stroller handle and took photographs with my free hand, the lens cap removed niftily by mouth. Bitsy had been strapped in for a while by the time the bell rang and she began to protest. I stretched over the stroller and unclipped her, just as Minky's teacher and a cluster of other parents walked purposefully past me towards the classroom steps. Maybe I misread our orientation material — maybe, or actually, I had not had time to read it before Bitsy drew rainbows all over it with eyeliner — but I didn't remember anything about an Informal Information Session in the classroom right after the bell. According to a helpful mother on her way up the stairs, that's what we were having.

'Oh, OK, I'll just go and get my other daughter,' I said, signalling towards Bitsy, who had run towards the play equipment.

'Do you want to leave your stroller here and I'll mind it while you go and get her?' the mother asked.

Sure, I *wanted* to, but that was beside the point. 'No, it's fine, I'll take it with me. Thanks, though!' I said, bouncing the empty carriage over the asphalt to hurriedly strap Bitsy back in.

'Here, let me lift that up the stairs for you,' a father said, pointing at the stroller as I joined the throng of parents waiting to walk up.

'It's fine!' I insisted, as he half-lifted it off the ground, my hand still wrapped tightly around the handle in a manner that he could only interpret as deep-seated distrust.

'OK, whatever you say,' he said, embarrassed by the rejection.

'All right!' the teacher said as we all walked into the classroom and looked around for little chairs to perch on. 'If I could just get you to leave any strollers outside, that might give us a little more space!'

I looked around. There was only one mother who had bumped a stroller upstairs, my good self. Everyone else with smaller children had left their $1,500 bugaboos parked outside. But this one, my actions seemed to say, this $50 beauty, I would *never* leave unguarded.

I waved goodbye to Minky at the end of the session, and Bitsy and I bumped back down the stairs and into the emptying playground. New mothers walked back to their cars crying into balled-up tissues; veterans scooted to and from the uniform shop; teachers tripped across the playground with piles of new exercise books; and Bitsy and I — well, we just looked at each other and she smiled, because suddenly, after two years in a trio, she had Mummy all to herself.

16

PERCH, THE SEQUELS

EVERY HOUSE WE RENTED AFTER BEBES I REMEMBER FOR ITS catalogue of faults, like a reverse property advertisement. 'TO LET' the notice would say. 'Two bedroom apartment with no storage, up perilous flight of concrete stairs. Nice natural light between 11.15 and 11.20 on a good day, unidentifiable smell in communal areas. References essential.'

We took photos of the nerds at home during this time and made little movies, but I never looked back at them, because I didn't want to revisit the dystopian vista of each home. Then, not so long ago, I needed to print out a baby picture for one of Minky's school projects and the search turned into a sort of nostalgic bender, Shab and I going through six years worth of photos and movie clips all at once.

I was surprised by what I saw. It all looked so … *nice*. That was not how I remembered it at all, being a glass-half-empty kind of person, for whom the glass is also chipped, so that it cuts my lip and gives me staph. Behind whatever toddler antic was being captured, I could see effort spent on making each apartment nice. There is always music on; the windows are clean and open; there are baking things laid out on the kitchen bench and children's art tacked up on the walls in a variety of non-bond-threatening methods (Japanese washi tape, not pins). And we all look so *happy* all the time. Nobody is screaming or crying, and I am always holding one of the nerds, kissing the other and laughing. All this time, I only remembered the rallying that went into making it feel that way, and how I would smile and talk constantly so that the girls wouldn't twig to all the insatiable yearning going on inside.

It is a sad reality for non-house-owning housewives that you have to turn your hand to whatever you get and just *make* it be nice. You scrub and decorate and assiduously pretend that this latest perch is home, even though all the pictures are leaning against the walls instead of being nailed into them. Then one day a landlord places a call and you're packing up the M*A*S*H 4077–style insta-home and moving on. You pretend, you un-pretend and then pretend again somewhere else. Maybe less demanding, less entitled women than me don't mind all that. Maybe they enjoy the fact that when you're renting and a pipe leaks it's not your problem. For me it always felt like essential, Sisyphean effort.

Eventually, though, two years after Russia, six years after babies, five years since London, something started shifting. A new wind began to blow. No Fruit Mondays became a bit more fruity, even it was just half a dozen waxy Granny Smiths rather than, say, your out-of-season berry fruit. Two months out of three, we didn't run out of money all that far from payday. I stopped having to choose between a magazine and a coffee and got both. If I got a parking ticket, I could work through the shame and despair in less than a week. Something was changing. Things weren't nearly as hard any more. Big and small advances were being made in the area of child development too: Bitsy was sleeping and, therefore, a much more likeable person during legitimate waking hours. Minky learned to do up her own seat belt and it seemed like a giant paradigm shift after so many years of craning into the back to do it for her. The nerds had started playing together too, which had been one of the major reasons for having more than one child in the first place, but during the sleepless years when Bitsy's two-pronged approach to interpersonal communication was screaming and scratching people's faces, the idea that they would ever get along had evaporated like a fever dream. Now there were little games with tea sets, cushions stuffed up dresses, imaginary doorbells and so much 'Let's make it that' and 'Let's 'tend.' Two days a week, both nerds were out of the house at their places of institutional care and I was free to read or write or cook something without holding someone on my hip at the same time. The thickest, greyest clouds that had hung heavily overhead for the past few years were shifting, burning off. Bright blue patches, life as it would one day be, were appearing everywhere.

And then, Golden Boy, the goldenest of all boys, reappeared with his beloved chequebook. After we had sold up in London, we had paid him back the original loan. He 'hadn't needed it', he said. 'It's still just sitting there, so if you want it again ...' I was glad at that moment we were on the phone, not Skype or anything, since I obviously needed to roll my eyes and do simultaneous pretend-barfing at the totally foreign and unbelievable notion that you could have more money than you needed. Anyway, he said, if we wanted to borrow it again, for another house, we could. Just holler, he said. I hollered, at him, then at Shab, then at nobody as I ran up and down the hallway. I hollered until I was hoarse. We could buy a house! Guys, we're not trying, we're buying; we're house hunting; we're looking for something. I couldn't believe it, no matter how many times I said it out loud or to myself as I searched property websites and websites that sold cushions and bedding and towels, everything I hadn't bothered to keep fresh stock of for all those years because I was living in that permanently suspended way that renting encourages. 'Why buy new towels when I don't even own a house?' went my self-punishing line of thought. Actually, fresh towels might have been just the thing, and I think I'm saying, with hindsight, buy the towels. Some comforts and small luxuries might have dulled slightly the sharp ache of a nesting instinct denied. Especially in the house I was then pretending was home. Although we had tripped through half a dozen incarnations of difficult accommodation since leaving London, the one we were living in that year was in many ways the most hostile to normal human activity.

We signed the lease because it was clean. Since so many dinners actually were eaten off the floor at the time, it was nice to find a rental house with floors so clean you could eat dinner off them. Strictly speaking, though, it wasn't a house so much as a corridor pretending to be a house. It was narrow: just room, room, room, with a long hallway down one side. If you lay across it, you could touch both walls at the same time, but it took 15 minutes to walk the length of it. Here's what you do a lot of in a house like that: walk up, down, up, down, like you're crewing a submarine. There was no room to turn left or right, so for two years, we only walked on a direct east–west axis. All four of us, which meant we were constantly banging into someone heading the other way, like Dr Seuss's obstinate Zaxes. There was no living room per se, only a small area where the hallway widened out before it turned into a galley-style kitchen (that naval trope again). The floors were done with shiny cream tiles, and the cream kitchen cupboards were as slick as wet mirrors. There was a stainless-steel dishwasher, a glass-fronted oven and double glass doors at the back, so one swipe of a sticky little hand and the kitchen looked like a dusted crime scene. I had to holster a bottle of Windex at all times so it didn't feel like we were living on the set of 'CSI: Miami'. The whole routine — the up-down, up-down, wipe wipe wipe — was getting a bit snoozy.

Plus, when we had dinner parties — which we did a lot once I decided to just get on with it and stop being embarrassed about our perches — and everybody was seated, there wasn't room for anybody to get out and go to the bathroom. Getting up and sitting down had to be a group decision. If somebody needed a glass of water, the guest nearest the sink had to lean back on two legs of their chair and fill a glass from the tap, and hand it back down the table. Eventually, I discovered that instead of passing bread around, it was easiest just to throw it like an American quarterback. Always get the baguette if you're hosting a dinner in a narrow semi; it's the most aerodynamic of breads.

The garden was even less usable than the pathology-lab-meets-subway-carriage kitchen. It was long and narrow too, of course, but very pretty and shaded by beautiful oak trees. The landlord had decided to cover the entire space with supposedly maintenance-free pavers. But between each paver, he left a gap of maybe five centimetres, which he filled with so many little white choky-choky ornamental stones and the odd spidery clump of mondo grass. The pavers were too far apart to take two at a time (that required a sort of bouncy skip if you were going to make it across) but too close for one at a time. One at a time forced you into a kind of clipped mincing. I loved watching Shab do the mincing; he'd always ham it up for effect. Meanwhile the oak trees turned out to be exceptionally dropsy, showering the garden with a permanent sprinkle of leaves and tiny acorns and twigs. Because of the stones, you couldn't sweep them up, but because it looked so neglected if you didn't, you had to pick them up somehow, and at least once a week. The only way to do it was with your two naked hands, while on a break from fingerprint duty. The children couldn't play or ride scooters out there. Nobody could even sit on a chair, because two out of the four legs would slip into the gravelly ditches. The only thing you could do out there was hang washing and try not to get a decorative rock embedded in your bare heel or let Bitsy swallow any while you reached into the peg basket. Cons.

Pros. It was fresh and renovated, on the leafiest street with the prettiest name. It was the first time we'd had a garden since we got married. It was the first time, actually, that I could be both outside and at home simultaneously. All the houses in the row had garages along a back lane, which meant the footpath out the front was free of driveways and baby-squishing Klugers. I could sit on the front step with a book and a cup of tea while the nerds scootered up and down the street playing a game of Let's Make It We've Got No Mum. Four doors down lived two other little girls the same age, minus an egg cycle or two, as Bitsy and Minky. For months, I was too nervous to say hello to their mother, because she drove a super-shiny 4WD and her house was double-fronted which meant that her more privileged children could walk in any direction they chose. But I should have learned, from Nona, about judging your neighbours by their blousons/houses, because as it so happened, Bel was a bebe-ignoring, loud-talking, coffee-sucking PLU, and soon we had another batch of street-besties. She was six months pregnant with her third baby the day we finally collided in the street, and within maybe five minutes, she offered to show me a throbbing varicose vein so high up her thigh she had to think about whether to give me a visual by pulling her shorts up, or down. She chose up and I had another keeper.

The children were old enough to run to and from each other's houses without supervision, as in some kind of suburban idyll. There was a trampoline at theirs and a rabbit at ours, two stonkingly novel entertainments depending on which family you belonged to and were already 'bored of'. When once Minky was invited over to jump on the trampoline while Bel sprayed everyone with the hose and made bubbles with washing-up liquid, she came home hours later, puffing, exhilarated, dripping from her baggy cossie, and declared that the entire episode had been 'a dream come true for me really, Mum'. Like Minky, Bel's oldest daughter was serious and responsible. The younger one, Bitsy's opposite number, was a fearless, feisty ragepot who made Bitsy look like one of Gina Ford's good case studies. The first time we had her over, she wandered down in a faded lilac Speedo swimsuit, chewing matching purple gum and twisting it around her little bitten nails painted with yellow polish. Bitsy was in love.

Bel's house had a large veranda across the front, which was always piled with shoes and pink bikes and bits of broken Christmas decoration in mid-April. The front door was always open, and on Saturday mornings the whole family sat on the front steps and ate croissants. One Saturday afternoon, I had just put lamb shanks into my imitation Le Creuset when I wandered out to get something from the car and met Bel on the front steps. We started chatting, the girls wandered down, the husbands appeared, champagne got opened, and when the shanks were done, we carried them from our house to theirs in the iron-hot Le Fauxset. They had some sourdough left over from something, so we ate that too and chatted and drank on the porch. We talked about property, being Sydneysiders and all, and they suggested we try the Inner West, where they'd lived as newlyweds. It was a good idea since all the North Shore houses that flicked up on my daily, sometimes hourly, property searches were about a million dollars too expensive, even with Golden Boy's advance. If we could afford one, it was about a million times too horrible. So we started looking on the other side of the bridge, where it's cheaper and edgier and pretty much the end of the earth if you're not from around those parts. Every Saturday morning we went house hunting. Guess what's not fun with bebes? That's right! House hunting is a hateful pastime without them, so with them, it's an exercise in anger management. Really, it combines the worst elements of any outing — carsickness, maps, overheating, hasty searches for public toilets — and there is no pleasant destination at the end. You do it all for hours every weekend to spend three minutes apiece in a series of ever-dumpier houses that smell like animals and cost $1.8 million. After six months of Saturday mornings like that, fruitless searches that kept ending in the not-buying of a house, my simmering desperation caught like milk in a pot and started to boil over. The dream, the sign that Phase 1, with all its hardship and longing and rallying and being strong and positive on such short rations, was finally over felt further away than ever. I went bananas. There'd been nothing like it since the bollard. It was a windy, greyish Saturday morning. The previous night, I had consumed a bottle of too-affordable red by myself and was suffering the cluster of symptoms — heavy eyes, biliousness and facial tic — that Nona refers to as Rosemount

Palsy. 'When we are better off,' Shab has since promised, 'we will buy wine that doesn't burn when you swallow.' In the meantime, we had to go look at three houses, all a 'level stroll to the airport', and I just couldn't. I couldn't even get in the car. *It was too much jobs! It was as boring as toast. It was totally grooted. Beyond Plathy. I hated it SO HARDLY. I was sick of my talkin' sounds! ONLY MORE SO.*

I cried, I yelled at Shab for some imaginary infraction and then I went quiet, which is, apparently, Shab says, quite a lot scarier than the first two. Sunday came and I was the same — the crying, the yelling, the staying in bed. Shab left for work on Monday, and although I pulled myself together a little, I kept railing. Tuesday, I stopped showering and eating. (Although, like catching a look at yourself in a mirror when you're crying and being secretly a bit pleased — eyelashes look *so* pretty wet — refusing food in a crisis is always a little self-conscious, I think. Crisis, sure, but losing weight, that's always nice.) I was at my end. I could hardly look at the girls, let alone mother them properly. I was desperate not only for a house — I would be a properly hateful human if this was really all just about the property ladder — but because, after Russia, I had let myself believe things would turn out. Now I felt stupid for it. Now it seemed that this was us forever — sad renters driving aimlessly around in their only asset, a rapidly depreciating Outlander. I cried for every day that I'd got up and got dressed, found something to do, chopped up fruit, read stories, pushed swings and fought off the darkest, loneliest thoughts that jostled for space in my head. Did that all count for nothing? Would I ever have a real, tangible sign that the long, hard drudge of it all would be redeemed? Had the rallying and the self-talk been for something, or had all our bad choices metastasised so that now, we could only wait for the end?

On Wednesday, Shab took the day off and ever so gently made me get out of bed. The girls were busy in their room so we sat at the kitchen table drinking tea beneath a heavy cloud of atmosphere.

'I don't think I can do this any more,' I said quietly. 'I think it's over.'

Shab started to say something, but I ploughed on.

'It's just been too hard for too long and I think ... I think I'm leaving you,' I said, truly meaning it. Shab sunk slightly in his seat, done in, and I stood up, my chair making a horrid shriek across the tiles. We looked at each other, not sure what to do next. It was unbearable. After a minute or two, Minky wandered into the kitchen.

'Go back to your room,' Shab said.

'I just need a drink,' she said.

'Minky, GO,' he said. She ran out, frightened, and we were alone again. I waited for him to do something. He just sat, looking at his hands.

'Come on then,' I said.

'What?' Shab asked, looking up.

'Well, I mean, you have to *come*,' I said. 'I can't really go without you.'

'So you're leaving me, but would like me to come with you?' he said.

'Yes.' I paused, aware that it was ridiculous, but what I really wanted. 'Because, I mean, I love *you*, I just hate all of *this*,' I said with a broad sweep of my arms designed to encompass the kitchen, the rest of our house, the car outside, our wider neighbourhood, Woolworths and its attendant car park, the half-dozen playgrounds in walking distance, our medical centre, the mingy soft-play place we only went to on rainy days, various hospitals and places of worship, the tricky intersection where you come off the bridge, his work, Sydney, Australia, the world, the universe.

'Me too,' he said. 'Where do you want to go?'

'Park?'

'Girls, get your shoes!' He stood up, grabbed the keys and we all walked out on us together and got Paddle Pops.

Bitsy and Minky ran off ahead and, as we followed behind, Shab put his arm around my shoulder and I was embarrassed because I felt like I didn't deserve it, or him, since I had let myself mistake the best thing in my life for the problem. When we got to the park, I watched Shab automatically wrap the stick of Minky's Paddle Pop in a napkin because she doesn't like the feeling of wet wood on her fingers and he knows it, and I vowed never to make that mistake again.

Oh, and also, it turned out I'd lost 500 grams, which was *awesome*. In the days that followed, I reached into the core of my miserable personhood for one last giant rally. I apologised so hardly to Shab for being such an epic shrew. He said, 'No sweat,' or something like it, and suggested we keep househunting for a bit longer. 'You never know,' he said. A few weeks later, I lay on my bed during Bitsy's rest time and opened up the property website that had been more heavily trafficked by moi that year than woolworthsonline.com.au and amidepressed.org put together. Up popped the prettiest perch my eyes had seen. I figured it had been filed in the wrong price bracket, because our money never meant anything pretty. It looked familiar but I couldn't place it. It looked like a child's drawing of a house, right down to the two symmetrical front windows and a front door below a red roof. It was missing only a child's incongruous additions of a bright yellow sun and smoke coming out of the chimney, but that didn't explain why I felt I knew it.

We went to look at it the following Saturday. I had learned with all strong starters not to go in, just in case the house was perfect and I couldn't have it. If ever I went inside, before I was back in the car, I would have imagined a hundred different sofa configurations and back-yard birthday parties and become deeply, painfully attached to a property that was destined for someone else. So Shab would go in and I would wait in the car with two hot, irritated nerds.

'So,' I said as he returned to the car. 'Any good?' Totally casual. Inside I was already burning with a hundred ideas about wisteria and puppies.

'It's small. It's really small,' he said. 'But you better go inside. Girls, Mum's just going to run in quickly.'

'To that one?' Minky asked, looking out the car window and through a thicket of other couples clutching brochures and single newborns, rather than two quite grown-up children. 'It looks like a doll's house for human people.'

'You know, I think it *is* a doll's house,' Shab said, trying to work out if the scale on the plans he'd been given could be correct. 'I think it's 80 square metres including the garden. That cannot be right.'

It was right, and it was perfect. To me. It wouldn't have been perfect to anyone with a different set of hopes and dreams. Someone who, for example, likes to buy the 12-pack of toilet tissue, because in a house of 80 square metres including garden, you can accommodate four rolls max unless you want to store the spares on your bedside table. To someone else, it would look like a wonky-floored workman's cottage, on two-thirds the scale of a normal house. In fact, it was just like one of those potato chip packets I was allowed to put in the oven when I was a child. The heat makes the packet shrink to a postage stamp–sized replica of a chip packet, and then you turn it into a key ring by drilling a whole in one corner — although, in my experience, it tends to shatter at that point into a dozen shards of molten plastic. Upon reflection, maybe Golden Boy and I were the only children let out to the shed to drill holes in boiling chip packets. 'So, I found you covered in melted plastic ...' Either way: it is the Chip Packet Perch. I am sitting here now. It is mine and I'm at the kitchen table, remembering everything that got us here. I know where I'd seen it before. The windows are the same, the front door is the same, the roof is the same colour as the plastic house Katya gave me, but this one is a tiny bit bigger and we can live in it. Bolognese is on the stove, and I am about to go and collect Minky from school, where she will wrap her seven-year-old arms around my waist as soon as she sees me. Then I will collect Bitsy from preschool, and when I walk in, she will pretend to be all like, whatever, because she's four and cool and my appearance could dilute the Bitsy brand. We are seeing Nona and her squirts (there are three of them now) for a Jat and a burn in the BPG, our old stomping ground, after school. I know what I have. Evidence of goodness, of redeemed-ness, is everywhere I look. Before I could really enjoy it, though, I had to just test it one more time, because, you never know, there may be some sort of prize and recognition of awesomeness at the end.

17

SO, I WENT BACK TO WORK!

LAST YEAR, WITH MINKY SIX AND BITSY THREE, I TOOK A JOB. It wasn't because I needed one. It wasn't even because I was bored, or that I'd felt the vicelike stricture of the 'What do you do all day?' question wind in even tighter. I took it because I was flattered that they asked me. Doing anything because the offer is flattering is almost always a mistake. 'Do you want to be the come-early person at my party?' a friend will sweetly ask and the next thing you know, you're making guacamole and uphill conversation with the friends-of-friends who arrived before their link person. 'We think you'd be an amazing addition to the P & C.' That's you manning a commercial barbecue three weekends out of four. And, of course, there is 'Will you be my bridesmaid?' In my case, it was 'We need somebody to cover for the managing editor for six months while she covers the editor's maternity leave.' And suddenly, the peaceful, not-even-sorry-any-more domestic bubble that it took me so many years to work out — well, I popped it. Although not before I accidentally told the outgoing editor who interviewed me that she was fat, right to her skinny face.

She was eight months pregnant and as thin as a python that had just swallowed a little fawn. As I walked into her glass office for my interview, she stood up to come and shake hands, but getting the baby deer between her desk and an adjacent board table required some difficult manoeuvring.

'Gosh, six more weeks and you won't fit through there! Har har!' I said, as I stepped forward to shake her outstretched hand. She withdrew it before I could get there, and stared at me, while the current managing editor, who had shown me in, waited to see how exactly I planned to make that comment OK.

'Someone else said I looked big this morning,' the editor said. 'And I just thought "Fuck you."' And me too, let's be honest.

I sat down in the chair opposite her and I really don't remember what happened after that. All I could think about was that I'd bought a tailored blazer for this, which I might as well cut down for Barbie clothes. Still, a day later, the managing editor called back.

'So, if you still want it, we'd love to have you,' she said.

'Really? But I flamed out so badly yesterday.'

'Yeah, well, ah …' She didn't deny it. 'You won't be working with her anyway, so it doesn't matter, does it?'

After six years, I had a job again. And a childcare problem, a wardrobe crisis and no real certainty that I could do all the things I may or may not have promised I could do after the 'Hey, fatty' opener. It was ironic, in a free-ride-when-you've-already-paid sort of way, that all this happened the week before we moved into the home for which I had been pining for so long. My chance to finally hang a painting or break my own windows without visualising a $3,000 bond swirling down the toilet was lost in the rush to find a nanny and bulk-buy black opaques.

I found a nanny called Milly, a medical student taking a year off and devoted Jane Austen fan who would, over the course of her tenure, explain the plot of *Pride and Prejudice* to my besotted children in such detail that Bitsy started using phrases like 'make haste' and 'vexing' in everyday life. Still when asked her age Bitsy will say she is 'but four years old' instead of just saying 'four' while holding up a nearly corresponding number of chubby fingers. After a few hours of handover ('These are Pine O Cleen Wipes. You can use them for *anything*.') Milly started and I went to work. To begin with, I liked it a lot. I had been out of full-time work, by then, for twice as long as I had ever been in it, and it was all unbelievably novel. Exactly as I had when I was first a mother, I felt like I was playing. I felt like a child in the preschool office corner doing bashy computering and talking into two phones at once. I used the phrases 'my nanny' and 'the nanny' as often as I could, just to see how they felt falling off the tongue. I'd never had a chance to say 'my obstetrician' or 'my builder' or 'the girl who helps me' even once during the lean years, so I had ground to make up. I felt a dizzy high now when someone asked me what I did all day. I courted that question and furnished the answer with one of a thick wad of business cards that never left my hand. 'Oh, I'm the managing editor of ___ magazine. And I have two daughters as well, so ...' It was all I could do to stop talking before I shouted 'GET ME!' in the inquirer's innocent face, wiping mine clear of spittle afterwards. The work was interesting. I went out on assignments and interviewed famous people, but it was the little luxuries of work that I liked best — getting coffee and drinking it hot, wearing nice clothes, basic things. Also, unlike being at home, where you're touched and sat on and pawed at all day, at work nobody is allowed to touch you. If they do, you get a massive payout. I had meetings. I liked meetings. I was in a meeting. I had to dash off to a meeting. I'd just got out of a meeting. That was all fun to say. I straightened my hair every morning and wore eyeliner, and nobody on the bus or in the coffee queue seemed to twig to the fact that this was all a giant have on my part, that I was an impostor and actually there was no-one on the other end of my phones.

That was the first week. The second week, the novelty started to fade. For years, I'd listened to working mothers talk about how hard the juggling is, how exhausting it is to balance work and babies, but stay-at-homers make it our business not to believe anything a working mother says. It's just part of the code — we listen, we nod and we try not to let judgement show on our faces. Tiny glitch, it's totally true. Being a working mother *is* hard. It is so hard. I remembered a story I'd read and discounted as a stay-at-home mother, by the *Sunday Times* columnist India Knight. She had interviewed a clutch of working mothers about how it was turning out for them, her central line of inquiry, 'Would you like your daughter to have a life like yours when she grows up?'

'If you asked a man the same thing about his son,' Knight wrote, 'the answer would probably be: yes, give or take the odd thing. But for mothers the case is usually different. For an increasing number of women, the answer now seems to be a resolute: "Absolutely not."' Because it's so hard, I realised now. The rushing, the stretching, the guilt, the feeling jealous of your nanny because she gets to kiss the hurts and buy the milkshakes while you earn money that you'll give, almost entirely, to her. I repented of every mean thing I'd ever thought about mothers who work. 'You don't know me,' I wanted to say to all the working mothers on my bus trying to clear emails on BlackBerrys they held up over their heads so that the toddler on their lap couldn't grab it, 'but my friends and I have been making some pretty harsh calls about you and your people — and, well, you were right this whole time. Working motherhood is really hard. I'm really, *really* sorry. You look really nice today by the way.'

Within a month or so, I was as tired as I'd been during Bitsy's period of permanent upness. Although as a mother I was used to thinking about 12 separate topics simultaneously, as a stay-at-homer the topics were all the same size and shape and carried the same degree of heft — what's for dinner, who has nits? Now, as a managing editor and a mother, my topics were all out of sync. Great big enormous worky problems sat beside domestic problems that were trivial in comparison but still fought for the same finite brain space. Will this story make a cover, will I meet this deadline, who has nits? I was permanently torn. Oh my goodness, is this what Spackers was talking about the whole time? I wondered one day. It was. Sometimes, when Shab asked how my day had been, I could only muster three lines of Natalie Imbruglia's single of the same name before falling asleep in my clothes. Nothing's fine, I'm torn, I'm all out of something, this is how I something …

My perpetually split focus showed itself in other ways too, particularly garbled speech and a consistent lack of preparedness.

So much work was required to get into the office, I couldn't think about actual work until I was physically there. And when I was, apparently, I couldn't talk good. Somewhere in the world right now is a well-known fashion designer who will always remember me as the journalist who introduced herself by pressing an entire wad of business cards into her hand and saying, 'Hi! I'm *really* nice to meet you.'

'Are you?' she replied, bewildered.

I wish I could have been better at it, all of it, and especially the bits involving Ewan McGregor. He was in Sydney promoting a film, and the magazine was offered time with him, 15 minutes at 1 p.m. on a Saturday. None of my child-free colleagues wanted to do it since they had other plans for Saturday, like sleeping and lighting fires with their disposable income. My plans for Saturday were preparing for Monday and trying to control Bitsy — who had become, ever since I'd started work, totally uncontrollable for the first half of the weekend — so I was happy to do it. By Saturday night, she'd remember that she did love me after all, that I wasn't bad people, but on that first day after five days away from each other, Bitsy needed to punish me. Even though her tactics — calling me Milly on purpose or refusing to eat breakfast because it didn't have a face made out of fruit on it, a Milly specialty — were hand-in-front-of-face obvious, they still worked. I felt terrible and had secretly begun to dread the beginning of each weekend.

The only currency I had was rubber gloves, because Bitsy was in the midst of a major latex-glove obsession at the time. Glubs were her reason for living, it would not be overstating things to say, and I could get her to do nearly anything by offering her two more from the dispenser box of 100 powder-frees I kept in a high cupboard. She crafted with them; she filled them with water and drank from them; she wore them on her feet and pretended they were flippers — their uses were literally untold. So that was our Saturday, a fraught, shouty, rubbery-smelling battle of wills.

Ewan-McGregor-Saturday was no different. Bitsy woke at 6 a.m., feisty and gunning for a tiff. She wanted glubs, but I wasn't about to hand over my only bargaining chip before it even got light. I said no, which compelled her to climb onto the kitchen table, shout, fall off and land on her wrist. I was too slow to catch her, I felt because my usually catlike maternal reflexes had been dulled by our daily separation. She sat up, paused for a split second, then burst into tears, cradling her floppy wrist. She couldn't move it, she said; it hurt, it hurt, it huuuuuuuuuuurt. She wouldn't let me touch it, ice it, or even look at it. It was 7 a.m. We decided to wait a while before we committed to a Saturday morning in the emergency room, since Saturday mornings in A & E mean school sports injuries and hours and hours of vending-machine coffee. By 8 a.m., she still refused to use her arm, so all four of us, me in my

Ewan-McGregor-meeting ensemble, got into the car and drove to the hospital. The waiting room was already jammed, and we were triaged behind a boy in a muddy soccer uniform whose nose lay across his cheek like a sleeping piglet. I toyed with the idea of asking the reception nurse to bump us up to the head of the queue because I had to be in the city by 1 p.m. to sit on an overstuffed sofa at the InterContinental and drink sparkling water out of a wineglass with the star of *Trainspotting* and all the new Star Warzes. 'There will always be bleeding children,' I wanted to say, 'but Ewan McGregor is only in Sydney for *twenty-four hours*.' She didn't look like the kind of nurse to go for it; so, instead, I sat reading a *New Idea* that had had its cover torn off, rubbing Bitsy's back and willing the doctors to hurry up. By 12.15, we had had an x-ray and seen a resident, a registrar and a physiotherapist, none of whom could quite tell what was wrong with Bitsy's wrist, which was still resting limply in her other hand five hours after her fall.

I was dressed for my interview but in no other way was I prepared for it. No questions were written; I hadn't done any deep background, a.k.a. Wikipediaering on my phone; and I was starting to get nervous. Shab promised that Bitsy would be fine without me, that I should just go and do the interview; he could manage Bitsy, and Minky, who was nearly unconscious with boredom by then. I should just call, he said, when I was done, since they'd probably still be waiting for the orthopaedic surgeon, who was making glacial progress towards us on his round.

I was riven with guilt. I *had* to go since it was a weekend and I couldn't track down another journalist and have them take my place. A small part of me wanted to do the interview since Ewan McGregor is kind of a big deal. I mean, he's no Matt Damon, but since Matt Damon and Shab remain interchangeable in my mind, having both chunked up and greyed a little since their *Bourne Identity* days, that's probably for the best. If I'd been sent to interview Matt Damon, there's a real chance I would have sat down, become confused and been all, 'Babe, those bins need to go out and Minky isn't wearing sun cream. Why are you just *sitting* there?' A larger part of me wanted to stay with Bitsy, but I kissed her goodbye and hailed a cab, promising myself I'd make the interview quick and dirty, ad-lib the whole thing and be back at the hospital within the hour.

It wasn't until I was in the lift climbing to the 33rd floor of the hotel that I remembered that I HADN'T SEEN ANY OF EWAN McGREGOR'S FILMS, just the first 15 minutes of *Down with Love* on an aeroplane and two episodes of *The Long Way Down* at my parents' house one Christmas. I had gone to the press screening of the movie he was in town to promote but it was really quiet and dark in the screening room, so I did what all mothers do in front of slow-moving ensemble pieces: I shut my eyes and went to sleep. I had nothing, but I was already being shown in to the suite by his brisk American publicist.

'Come over here!' Ewan exclaimed as I walked in. *Gosh*, he's pretty. 'Come and look at this amazing view.' He was standing by a floor-to-ceiling window that framed the entire harbour.

'Isn't it beautiful? Well, apart from this,' he said, slapping the thick, black window frame that bisected the glass and blocked out the middle of the bridge.

My lack of preparation and inability to talk good had tripped me up in professional situations before, and that was when I wasn't totally starstruck. This was going to be huge. I still hadn't said anything, even though by now we were standing shoulder to shoulder admiring the view.

'What do you think?' Ewan asked, his (beautiful, manly) hand still resting on the window frame.

'Well, yes, it's lovely apart from that,' I said, too stiffly. I had to loosen it up so that he stayed chatty. 'Can't you just call reception and' — this is when I imitated Ewan McGregor in front of Ewan McGregor — 'be all "Don't you know who I am! I'm kind of a big deal. Send someone up here to move this pillar!"'

His eyes widened. The magazine had sent him a loon! He exchanged quick, meaningful looks with his publicist, who knew to be on high alert for the rest of this interview. Ewan directed me to the sofa and offered me a San Pellegrino, and

I flicked on my digital recorder, so glad I hadn't taped myself coming in and out of a Scottish accent minutes earlier.

'So!' I said, hoping he'd just sense my unpreparedness and go ahead and reveal stuff while I taped it.

'So!' he said back.

'This must get boring! All these interviews!' I said.

'I don't mind, really. I'd be a bit of a tosser to complain about my job,' he replied. Gosh, he was just *so* pretty. His T-shirt was a whiter shade of white than I'd ever seen on a civilian, a sort of digitally enhanced white that made his ... whoa, I'd forgotten to answer again.

'Mmm. So the film is great ...' I saw his eyes glaze over. I was probably the tenth journalist to try that line today. It was time for the big, desperate guns.

'Listen. I'm a really bad interviewer,' I said. 'It's a joke in the office, actually, how bad I am. I promise you, when I listen back to this tape it will be 90 per cent me making lame jokes, so let's just not do it and say we did. Let's just chat until my time is up.'

'All right,' said Ewan, baffled. 'That sounds fun.'

'So, you have three daughters, right?' I said. 'I have two. One of them is in hospital right now. I think she has a broken arm, but I'm here with you, which is a bit grooted. I mean rooted.'

This is the part where Ewan McGregor bumped Matt Damon from his long-held position in my mind as the bestest, nicest, movie star in the world. He chatted for 15 minutes about raising daughters, about family life, fame, Birkin bags, his wife, about missing them when he was away. 'Although when I am at home, I'm an extremely hands-on dad,' he said, after the publicist signalled that our time was nearly up. 'It's not like I get back from three months on set and I'm one of those dads who's all ...' He paused to imagine what a normal dad is like. 'A dad who's all ...'

'Poor?' I said.

'Quite!' Ewan laughed, shook my hand, and looked me in the eyes. 'This has been very strange.'

I was out the door and dialling Shab before I hit the lifts.

'How is she? Have you found out what's wrong?' I asked.

'I have.' There was a note of sad acceptance in his voice.

After another hour of waiting, five hours altogether, the orthopaedic surgeon had come and examined Bitsy and even he couldn't work out what was wrong. He sent Bitsy back for another x-ray, and then the resident came back to look at the results. He clipped the x-ray onto the light box and Bitsy watched from her spot on Shab's lap.

'Well, perhaps it's the angle of the x-ray,' the resident explained, 'but we're really unable to determine at this point ...'

Bitsy stretched up to whisper in Shab's ear. 'When is he going to do proper doctoring?'

'What do you mean, Bits?' Shab replied.

'When is he going to get out some glubs?'

Shab swallowed. 'I don't suppose,' he asked the resident, 'you could put gloves on for a second, could you? I think I might know what's wrong.'

The resident obliged, and as soon as he snapped them on and touched Bitsy's hand, she slid off Shab's lap, let go of her wrist and smiled warmly at the doctor.

'I all better now. We can go home, Daddy.'

The doctor offered her a sticker, but she waved him off as if to say 'yeah, I'm all good.' She had got her prize. The three of them pulled up just as I was paying my cab driver and we tripped up the front path like a vanquished army, just back from battle, me barefoot and holding high heels in my hands, Shab exhausted but hyper from hospital coffee, Minky loopy for attention and Bitsy, typical Bitsy. There was not a lot of joy in working motherhood for me, it seemed, only survival. Our Saturday was spent; our Sunday would be a blur of prep for the week ahead. We were losing what we had built. Every week, a little bit more slipped out of my hand. I couldn't see the point of it, even if that Pellegrino had been especially bubbly. The nerds were constantly in deficit, so I had to find the emotional reserves to be nice to them *after 5.30 p.m.* instead of just gunning out orders like I usually would at that time of day. For at-homers, nice is a morning thing. For working mothers, it has to last the entire time they're awake. Shab was becoming a semi-stranger whose sole function, as far as I could see, was to generate washing. Only once in the entire time did he make it home before me to untangle the children, debrief the nanny, empty school bags and refill them for the morrow.

I missed Bitsy and Minky in a way that felt physical like grief, but walking in the door at 6.30 p.m. to find them tired but awake, wild in their need for me, made me wish I'd stayed longer in the office so I could come home to them clean and sleeping. It should have been the other way — the more time I spent away from them, the more desperate I should have been to see them, but instead, the reverse seemed to be true. I was losing my mothering muscle and felt increasingly unable to deal with them at all. Milly was lovely, kind and good at her job, but I couldn't ask a woman who was already making my children's dinner, wiping it off the floor, helping them in the bathroom and holding a gun to their heads while they tidied their room, to please also write down everything they did and said so that I didn't feel utterly disconnected from them for five days out of seven.

The only thing that got written down was a lot of instructions in The Milly Book, a dog-eared exercise book from the News-Asian that I filled with notes and requests and errands for her. I have kept it in case I am ever flattered in this direction again and have forgotten how joyless and so much jobs it all is. 'Milly, half-made bol in that pot on stove. Could you get rest of ingreds and finish it? Bitsy went to bed at 10 last night, think she is tempy, so maybe no zoo today? Minky has to finish volcano proj this afternoon — need new cardboard because she smudged titles and screwed up other one. Sorry. Won't be home until seven tonight, is that OK? let me know if not. Sorry. Help self to that cake. x x oh and thanks for getting dry-cleaning. Pay self back with my card?'

It doesn't sound so fun. Every entry I'm sorry for ten different things, because I was worried about overloading her and embarrassed about having a non-Mason observe our day-to-day life from such close quarters, even though Milly was discreet about it. In fact, I think she was a little embarrassed too, it being her first nannying job and all, and not a profession she'd grown inured to. Case in point, the problem of Shab's underpants. I didn't make her do laundry. Instead, I ran the machine at night and hung the washing out in the pitch-black midnight, hoping it would dry the following day — but if it rained when I was at work, Milly would rescue it from the line. Everything except Shab's underpants. Either she couldn't bring herself to or she wasn't sure I'd want her to touch them. She took in everything else and left all the boy pants hanging from their corners, at random intervals, like dead bats suspended from power lines.

'Don't mind if you bring <u>everyone's</u> underwear in — it's v. helpful!' I wrote finally in The Milly Book.

'Have figured out,' she wrote back, 'how to do it without touching! Just kick basket under each and unpeg. They drop straight in, no hands!'

There was a deeper embarrassment too, something to do with paying another woman to be me, knowing that she couldn't call on the deep reserves of love that got me through each day. I knew how hard it is when you do love them, so how hard must it be when you don't? Once during a lunch hour, I snuck out to a cheap nail place with a workmate for pedicures. It was the exact thing I'd imagined doing in all my years at home daydreaming about the unimaginable freedoms of paid work, but as I sat in my giant vinyl throne and watched the miserable, round-shouldered Thai girl pull on a pair of glubs for the massage bit, all I could think about was paying people to do things that people who love you would do for free. She gazed out the window at the passing traffic while robotically running her hands up and down my arches and trying, I imagine, not to think about it. It was about the furthest thing from a loving human interaction I could imagine, and I wondered why I was paying someone to simulate the maternal equivalent.

It wasn't quite the dream. If you're a stay-at-home mother and still apt to glamorise work, if you're having a bad day with the babies and thinking, 'If only I could spend the day with adults! And wear nice clothes! And be rewarded for my toil. That would be so much better than this,' well, let me blow the lid off that big jar of foozy for you. Adults are more of a pain in the ass than children. They are just as needy and irritating, but whereas children would just throw sand at you and move on, an adult will fester and scheme. Maybe adults don't pull at your clothes when they want you to accompany them somewhere, but that is literally the only ongoing upside of office life. In the end, it's just extra work for money you don't get to keep. It is bulk tea bags, commuting and losing your pass, and if you didn't have a bottomless clothing budget before, you won't have one now. It's inventing five different ways with a Country Road tulip skirt instead of five ways with sag-kneed leggings. Towards the end I was toying with the idea of leggings on the bottom, Country Road tulip skirt on top as a kind of bustier; I had worn it every other way.

I thought it would never finish. And then it did. I lasted eight months, two whole months more than I signed on for upfront. The day I came home, a bunch of flowers in my arm and a little boosted stationery in the bottom of my work bag, Minky and Bitsy were waiting for me on the front steps, sitting in front of a sign they'd made and stuck on the front door. It said 'Congratulations' — giant 'CON', slightly smaller 'G' and then a 'ratulations' that sloped down to nothing. I dropped my keys, flowers and bag full of Sellotape dispensers on the front step, went inside, and we collapsed in a big armsy-legsy pile on the living room floor. It turns out our new neighbourhood is safer than I thought, because I forgot to go back outside to get everything and it sat untouched on the doorstep until Shab got home, even though there was literally $300 worth of office supplies on offer.

'No more jobs, ever, ever, ever, girls, I promise,' I said.

'Good,' said Bitsy, with her slightly dreadlocked working-mother hair falling in my face. 'Because when you're at work it makes me feel crooked and crunchy and angry.'

Dinner time came and we made burgers. It was high summer and still warm out, so we wrapped them up with wax paper and rubber bands and ate in the park at the end of our street. Minky unwrapped hers and held up the rubber band. 'Oh, I didn't know my burger came with a free toy,' she said, joking. I laughed. It wasn't personal-best funny or anything, but I was there to hear it. I hadn't missed it. The next day, I balled up my now-faded tulip skirt and the smart blazer and pushed them to the back of my wardrobe. My last travel pass expired, and I breathed a giant sigh of relief every time a city-bound bus full of workers went by us on our way to the local shops, or, as Bitsy now called them, Meriton, after the village in *Pride and Prejudice*.

This is our day now. In the school holidays, Shab leaves for work and the three of us stand on the steps and shout 'Sorry about that' as he runs for the bus. We go back to bed with green tea (one hot, two tepid) and read stories until we get hungry or hot or Bitsy does a forward roll on Minky and kicks her in the face by accident. We get dressed, shove rice cakes, water bottles, chalk, bubble mix and sunscreen in a bag. If Nona is perching, we go there. Otherwise, we go to the beach or the Botanical Gardens. We come home and I read while they watch an episode of *Pride and Prejudice* (Colin Firth edition, not Keira 'I just swallowed my own sick' Knightley edition). We eat Bolognese; they go to bed. In term time, we drop Minky at school, then Bitsy and I, we just hang. We get a milkshake; we look at the bookshop; we visit Bonus Granny and I listen to her soothing oratory while Bitsy fills the pond with gravel. I'm there when she trips over her own flip-flops and I catch all the funny things she says too. 'Your bozzies don't have milk in them any more, do they, Mum? Only park bark.' I am jealous for the time she and I lost while I was at work and when she was a difficult, nocturnal baby who demanded more loving patience than I ever had. Now I cannot see her or touch her or smell her enough. I carry her constantly, just because I can. Even though she has just turned five and is all legs, I haul her everywhere on my hip — we're like Katie Holmes and Suri Cruise, if Suri Cruise's signature look involved more medical latex than infant stilletos.

As Bitsy's fifth birthday approached, I thought back to the only party I had ever thrown for her and decided it was time to try again. We drew up a list of all our family friends and arrived at a number that would turn the Chip Packet Perch into a tiny mosh pit. Bitsy wanted a night-time party with pizza and dancing and chocolate sundaes. We bought sparklers, champagne and ice cream and we decorated the garden with fairy lights and helium-filled glubs. It was a clear winter's night, and at 6 p.m., our friends started pouring in. We — Minky, Shab,

Bitsy and I — danced for hours with all our friends, the real-life, non-plastic people we had collected since we came home. Snooch made a two-storey chocolate cake covered with edible farkles and Bitsy's eyes nearly popped out of her head when she saw it. There was no rallying, there was just being happy.

In a few months, Bitsy will start school and I won't go to a playground on a weekday morning ever again. I will have six manless, childless hours to fill every day in that invisible way my mother did with classic novels and being on the phone. My being at home will seem even less legitimate to the outside world than it did when I was at least required in a lactate-ory capacity. But other women on the beach with me will agree when I say, because I have just discovered it, that 'I actually think it's *more* important that I'm home now than it was when they were babies,' the sister statement to the 'Even if I go back to work when they're at school, the main thing is to be here for the baby years' of 2003. Then we'll laugh, those mothers and I, and we'll complain about all the homework — oh, the homework! — although, honestly, it's like five minutes of spelling and a home reader and we hardly ever do it. Maybe sometimes in the car if there's traffic, but otherwise we're as free as birds.

Still, I'll never go for a swim by myself or lie on my bed and read in the morning, because those things aren't fun when they're not stolen from the constant, looming threat of interruption. I will probably never again throw a Woolworths

Buffet or try to cram some work into nap time, anticipating the always-jarring post-nap cry. I'll never pick a rosy-cheeked baby up out of the cot, smiling and cooing while thinking, '*Damn*, I have two hours of things to do and now they will have to wait until tomorrow, plus it's only 1.50 p.m. and that is too early to start afternoon topics, because the park doesn't fill up until three and it's horrible being first in, but if I let you watch television now I will have used up all the afternoon telly points and how will I cook dinner?' I will be out at times of the day when, for years, I made myself be in. Anything — nuclear meltdown, peasant uprising — could have happened outside at 1 p.m. in the middle part of the last decade and I wouldn't have known about it, because 1 p.m. was nap time. Soon it will be just 1 p.m. again. To begin with, this will feel as strange and unknown as the day I first walked back into my West Kensington perch with a three-kilo Minky in my arms.

But I will worry about that next year. I'll find something to do, even if it's a new kind of made-up. I just want to unpack the appley-smelling school bags and find the super important school notices that are down the bottom and coated in yoghurt. I want to be the one who gets shouty when they won't get ready for swimming lessons, who finds a perfect circle of ham on the bathroom floor and takes care of it, who stands in front of the washing machine emptying sticks and gravel out of uniform pockets. I would also like to try some new ways with mince.

There is a children's book from the 1930s innocently, unfortunately titled *Woody, Hazel and Little Pip*. It's so wordy I would always turn two pages at once before the nerds were old enough to notice, and it's old-fashioned enough to contain a bunch of ideas that don't sit quite right with our modern sensibility — naked children in the forest befriending angry gnomes who try and sell them poison, and things like that — but it has the nicest last line of any book I've ever read. When Woody, Hazel and Little Pip, who get lost in the story, are finally found and come home, their mothers throw a party to celebrate. Something hard and horrible and thrilling has just finished, and something surely as hard and horrible and thrilling is just around the corner. In the meantime there is elderflower wine and dancing and children playing in the trees until way after bedtime. 'And so,' the writer says, 'our story ends, just when everything is at its best.'

REFERENCES

Chapter 2: An End, a Beginning

'The thing about Africa …' Martha Gellhorn, *Travels with Myself and Another*, Eland, London, 1978, p. 211

'Oh, for God's sake, Lucy …' written by Rodrigo Garcia, *Mother and Child*, Sony Picture Classics, 2009

Chapter 6: And Do You Work or …?

'I mean, don't get me wrong …' Ruth Jones and James Corden, 'Gavin & Stacey', Baby Cow Productions for BBC Wales, 2009

Chapter 9: Home. Help.

'When she is with them …' Rachel Cusk, *A Life's Work*, Fourth Estate, London, 2002, p. 7.

'Thyroiditis got you down?' Heidi E. Murkoff, Sandee E. Hathaway and Arlene Eisenberg, *What to Expect When You're Expecting*, Simon & Schuster, London, First edition 1984, my edition 2002, p. 414.

Chapter 17: So, I Went Back to Work!

'Would you like your daughter …' India Knight, 'Having it all is a myth girls, so just make sure your daughters marry rich men', *Sunday Times*, 17 May 2009.

THANK YOU

All the heavenly mothers I have met along the way who've made this experience more bearable, hilarious or more properly executed: Suzanne Mynors, Emma Birney Cunningham, Keren Fuller, Anna Smith, Nellie Evans, Rachel Page, Tiffany Zehnal, thank you. And thank you especially to Fiona Bateman, the reason for all the frenzied searching and the sign that it was finally over.

Kate Gibbs, only more so; you are an angel with a table and I am so grateful for your constant being-there-ness. Loren Taylor, I'm so happy you're back. Thank you Graeme and Bronny Hughes, Tim Walton and Ben and Clare Irons for cape-worthy acts of support and generosity in the very deserty bits. And word to my nerdminders, Lucy Woodhouse, Jo Mason, Gus and Anna Mason, Alex Orange, the grandparents real and bonus; because you did craft with my children, I didn't have to and I am full of gratitude, still.

A horribly overdue thank you to Anne Spackman for teaching me that 'all life is copy' and Michael Hunter, Justine Cullen, Danielle DeGail, Sara Mulcahy, Claire Bradley and Ceri David for professional inspiration and support throughout my happily checkered career.

At HarperCollins Australia, or Harper-Mr-Collins if you're Bitsy, I owe everything to the dynamic, inspiring Fiona Henderson, as well as Mel Maxwell, Kelly Fagan, Karen-Maree Griffiths and the brilliant Vanessa Mickan. Thank you ladies.

And to all the mothers who came after me, Louisa Davies, Sarah Wimpress, Alexis Greeves, Allie Beckett, Claire Bernard, Simcha Hutton, Jo Kay and Amber Hawkes, without whom this book was sadly possible — I wish so much I'd had you all from the start but I'm so glad you're on the beach now.

Finally, Shab, and the real Bitsy and Minky. What would I have to say without you?

ABOUT THE AUTHOR

Meg Mason is the creator of the popular 'Mum Vs World' column in *Sunday Magazine*. The New Zealand-born writer began her career at the *Financial Times* in London before switching to *The Times* to write lifestyle, parenting and humour. After relocating to Sydney, she began writing for the *Sydney Morning Herald*, *Russh*, *The British Medical Journal*, *Cosmopolitan*, *Shop Til You Drop* and *GQ*. She lives in Sydney with her husband and two daughters. When she is not writing, she is reading.